THE
GUINNESS BOOK
of
HUMOROUS
SPORTS QUOTES

Colin Jarman

GUINNESS PUBLISHING

Walter L. McKone DO, MRO

*The man with healing hands and miraculous feats; always
remember that laughter is the best sports medicine!*

Michael O'Shaughnessy DO' AFC

*The man who thinks a cardiologist is a professional
poker player – read it and weep! Hawajiss at last!*

First Published 1996
Reprint 10 9 8 7 6 5 4 3 2 1 0
Published in Great Britain by Guinness Publishing Ltd,
33 London Road, Enfield, Middlesex

Front cover illustrations, courtesy of Allsport UK Ltd:
Will Carling (David Rogers), Eric Cantona (Anton Want),
Nigel Mansell (Pascal Rondeau), Michael Atherton (Ben
Radford). Chris Eubank by All Action (Gareth Davies).

Design and layout: Moondisks Ltd, Cambridge
Printed and bound by Cox & Wyman Ltd,
Reading, Berkshire

'GUINNESS' is a registered trademark of
Guinness Publishing Ltd

A catalogue record for this book is available from
The British Library

ISBN 0–85112–627–8

Contents

"Introduction"

Just as James Greaves Esq. forever reminds us,

'It's a funny old game',

this volume of humorous sports quotes echoes his much-lampooned sentiment in kind.

This is my second *Guinness Book of Sports Quotations*; the first, published in 1990, covered every aspect of sport from Ancient to Modern. This sequel, of sorts, concentrates solely on the humorous aspect of sport.

As former Oakland Raider, Gene Upshaw, once said,

'If you didn't have humour, you couldn't have sport.'

So,

if humour be the food of sport, play on ...

Colin M. Jarman

"Athletics"

IN A MOMENT, WE HOPE TO SEE THE POLE VAULT OVER THE SATELLITE.

David Coleman, BBC TV (1976)

Break Fast Of Champions

When I lost my decathlon world record I took it like a man. I only cried for ten hours.

Daley Thompson (1980)

On Moses Kiptanui breaking eight minutes for the 3,000 metres steeplechase – Moses finds the promised land.

***The Observer* headline (1995)**

Decathinated

The decathlon is nine Mickey Mouse events and the 1500 metres.

Steve Ovett

Being a decathlete is like having ten girlfriends. You have to love them all, and you can't afford losing one.

Daley Thompson

As a runner Daley Thompson is excellent, as a jumper he is excellent, and as a thrower he is an excellent runner and jumper.

Cliff Temple (1978)

Behind every good decathlete, there's a good doctor.

Bill Toomey

I spent 12 years training for a career that was over in one week. Joe Namath [New York Jets] spent one week training for a career that lasted 12 years.
Bruce Jenner

Drug Bust

Without the use of drugs our athletes are like drivers of a racing car with one gear less than their rivals.
Harvey Smith (1967)

It should not have surprised anyone that Ben Johnson was using steroids. You don't go from 10.17 [seconds] to 9.83 on unleaded gas.
Jamie Astaphan (1989)

On the reduction of his drug ban – Ben Johnson must still be the fastest human in the world. He served a lifetime sentence in just two years.
Mike Littwin *Baltimore Sun*

My son Linford does not use drugs. If they said he was taking roast chicken and baked potatoes then I would believe that.
James Christie (1988)

You have to be suspicious when you line up against girls with moustaches.
Maree Holland (1988)

If Diane Modahl was 40 times over the testosterone limit she'd have a deep voice and we'd all be calling her Barry White.
Tony Jarrett (1994)

On his wife Diane's drug ban – It is like being told Pavarotti has been using someone else's voice.
Vicente Modahl (1994)

Gold Rush

After Sergei Bubka asked for $40,000 to appear at a Crystal Palace meeting – Sergei, I'm only asking you to compete, I don't want to buy the Soviet Union.
Andy Norman (1987)

They are prepared to pay Ben Johnson and Carl Lewis ridiculous sums, but promoters want me to come on Oxfam.
Linford Christie (1988)

On the £20,000 Mercedes prizes for each winner at the World Athletics Championships in Stuttgart – Anyone good enough to win already has one.
Michael Johnson (1993)

High Her Dolls

Italian men and Russian women don't shave before a race.
Eddie Ottoz

I have observed in women of her type a tendency to regard all athletics as an inferior form of fox hunting.
Evelyn Waugh *Decline and Fall* **(1928)**

The 880-yard heel and toe walk is the closest a man can come to experiencing the pangs of childbirth.
Avery Brundage (1956)

Kit And Kaboodle

They may have helped Linford Christie shave a millisecond or two off his personal best but not everyone is Linford Christie. And contour-hugging cycle shorts can cruelly expose anyone whose performance falls an inch or two short of an all-comers' record. You need a full kitbag to get away with this particular garb. That might explain why so many men wear their cycle shorts *under* their regular strip.

Richard Littlejohn *Punch* **(1992)**

I am still looking for shoes that will make running on streets seem like running barefoot across the bosoms of maidens.

Dave Brosnan

Leap Yore

On the 1968 Olympic steeplechase champion – Amos Biwott leaped the water jump as if he thought crocodiles were swimming in it.

Joe Henderson (1968)

On Sing-Sing Prison's athletics day – We do not have cross-country and we do not have pole-vaulting.

Gerald Curtin

My first 18-foot pole vault wasn't any more of a thrill than my first clearance at 15 or 16 or 17 foot. I just had more time to enjoy it on the way down.

Roland Carter (1976)

On his success in the Superstars *TV programme* – I still think I could be the best pole vaulter in Britain, but I'm in danger of falling between two stools.

Brian Hooper (1982)

On her Olympic Pentathlon winning performance – Sheila Sherwood told me that I blew so many kisses to the crowd after every jump that I could have got the job at the very end of *The Morecambe and Wise Show*.

Mary Peters (1972)

I always wanted to be a minor poet. I remember when I did my record long jump saying to myself, when I was in the air half-way, 'This may be pretty good jumping. It's dashed poor minor poetry!'

C. B. Fry

Plainly no way has yet been found to stop long-jump commentaries sounding like naughty stories after lights-out in the dorm – 'Ooooh! It's enormous. It was so long!'

Russell Davies *The Sunday Times*

On his world record triple jump – It's only jumping into a sandpit.

Jonathan Edwards (1995)

Long Distance Runaround

You don't run 26 miles at five minutes a mile on good looks and a secret recipe.

Frank Shorter

Finland has produced so many brilliant distance runners because back home it costs $2.50 a gallon for gas.

Esa Tikkannen (1979)

Before winning the London Marathon – I hope to be the fastest fat old git in the race.

Eamonn Martin (1993)

To describe the agony of a marathon to somebody who's never run it is like trying to explain colour to a person who was born blind.

Jerome Drayton (1977)

On being asked if having 'tree trunks for legs' was a disadvantage in the marathon – Not unless they have Dutch elm disease.

Rob de Castella

If you want to know what you'll look like in ten years, look in the mirror after you've run a marathon.

Jeff Scaff

Scratch marathoners once – they tell you how wonderful they feel. Scratch them twice and they tell you about their latest injuries.

Arnold Cooper (1981)

After Bill Rodgers won the Boston Marathon – It's good to have a guy running in my district that I don't have to worry about.

Senator Joseph Moakley of Boston

Newtrition

The French cannot produce great track-and-field teams like they can produce great wines for probably that reason: the winemakers got in first.

Michael Lourie (1980)

Anon US interviewer: I suppose you'll have a drink?
Guy Drut *(after winning the Olympic high hurdles)*: Certainly. I will have a Lafite Rothschild 1964.

Ready, Get Sex, Go!

I never developed the macho side as a lot of boys do. Even my sister, Carol, shows more masculinity, but that doesn't make me a homosexual. They say I am, but I am not. They say it because nobody knows what I'm doing. I don't even sleep in the same hotel as the other athletes. I could be sleeping with a horse, for all they know.

Carl Lewis (1987)

On being asked if there would be any late night goings-on during the Olympics – I certainly hope so.

Kate Schmidt

On a report which revealed today's youth put sex as their number one sport – It seems today's youngsters have one-track minds. Unfortunately it's not the athletics track.

Anon spokesman (1994)

Run, Rabbit, Run

Running is an unnatural act, except from enemies and to the bathroom.

Anon

A cross-country runner is a landscape panter.

Anon

S.A.S. (Steve And Seb)

During a photo-call with fellow Olympic gold medallist Duncan Goodhew – Pity Steve Ovett didn't show up. Then we could have had the good, the bald and the ugly.

Daley Thompson (1980)

There is no path I follow. I feel as if I'm just drifting along, because although I can progress physically, through my training, mentally and spiritually I don't know what the hell I'm doing. It's like that car sticker: 'Don't follow me, I'm lost'.

Steve Ovett (1978)

Seb Coe is a Yorkshireman. So he's a complete bastard and will do well in politics.

Daley Thompson (1993)

L'Huomo Dull personified. Seb Coe in a C & A V-neck is like a square peg in a round hole.

Peter Freedman *Glad to be Grey* **(1985)**

Speed Merchants

Only think of two things – the gun and the tape. When you hear the one, just run like hell until you break the other.

Sam Mussabini

Linford Christie: the generously-beloined sprint supremo.

Punch

There's nothing new you can say about Linford Christie – except, he's slow and has got a small penis.

Nick Hancock *They Think It's All Over* **BBC TV (1995)**

On Carl Lewis's short-lived ponytail – He looks like the love child of Grace Jones and Paul Revere.

Tony Kornheiser *Washington Post* **(1990)**

Carl Lewis: Mr Smarm – the interviewer's dream (though by all accounts, a bit of a madam in his dealings with other athletes).

Andy Lyons *Melody Maker* **(1988)**

On Carl Lewis stepping up to the 800 metres – He thinks he'll be happier in the long run.

Frank Litsky

I wouldn't be surprised if one day Carl's halo slipped and choked him.

Allan Wells (1989)

Don't talk about Michael Johnson's style. Look, if that guy ran with his fingers up his bum he could still run 42 seconds.

Roger Black (1995)

Throw Up

Mention that you are a hammer thrower to someone who is not an athletics enthusiast and you will be met with any reaction from a puzzled frown to raucous laughter. If you have the misfortune to say it to a groundsman, you may face physical violence.
Howard Payne

I don't think the discus will ever attract any interest until they let us start throwing them at one another.
Al Oerter

I know I'm no Kim Basinger, but she can't throw a javelin.
Fatima Whitbread (1993)

On news of a new throwing style – If this new method is accepted I will personally break my javelin in half and use it as a support for my tomato plants.
Dana Zatopekova (1956)

After being impaled by a javelin, while officiating – I'm doing fine now, just resting and hanging around.
Jeremy Campbell

A shot-putter is the power behind the thrown.
Journolists *Mail on Sunday*

Wonder Meant

I have always sensed the exhilaration and independence of being self-propelled. Besides, you can jog while pushing a baby carriage. Maybe I'm a product of Wonder Woman comic books
Nina Kucsik

It always makes me laugh,
It's such a wonderful treat:
To see an athlete run a mile
And only move two feet
Anon

Animal Instinct

*On Jack Dempsey winning the world
heavyweight title* – The champion, Jess
Willard, had about as much chance in
this fight as a dish-faced chimpanzee in a
beauty contest.
Arthur 'Bugs' Baer (1919)

Jumbo Cummings – a name that sounds
like an elephant ejaculating.
Rory McGrath *They Think It's All Over*
BBC TV (1995)

*Before Alan Minter's successful world
title fight against Vito Antuofermo* –
Minter thinks that yielding is a term used
to describe the going on racecourses.
Hugh McIlvanney (1980)

Ballet Hoo

If a boxer ever went as crazy as Nijinsky
all the wowsers in the world would be
screaming 'punch drunk!' Well, who hit
Nijinsky? And why isn't there a campaign
against ballet? It gives girls thick legs.
A. J. Liebling *The Sweet Science*

*After her son Johnny had been banned
for life for hitting a referee* – I wish I had
put ballet shoes on him and not boxing
gloves.
Hazel Frankham (1987)

Below The Belt

My girlfriend boos when we make love because she knows it turns me on.
Hector Camacho (1989)

After his heavy defeat by Matthew Saad Muhammad – I'm going down so often these days you'd think I was making a blue movie.
John Conteh (1980)

Contrary to the old wives' tale that bloody-minded trainers put around, a little love-in before the main event can do you more good than a rub-down with *The Sporting Life*.
John Conteh

It's strange … two guys in shorts competing for a belt. They should, at least, award them slacks or a shirt.
Jerry Seinfeld *Seinlanguage* (1993)

Biblical

At the weigh-in for the big fight tomorrow, Goliath tipped the scales at 15 stone 3 pounds, and David at 14 stone three pounds. David's manager said this evening, 'The odd stone could make all the difference.'
John Cleese *I'm Sorry I'll Read That Again*

Sport is business and business is business. It's nothing really new – Kid Cain would not have put his title on the line against Boy Abel if the money hadn't been right.
Frank Keating

I just visualise fighting as a sport, no worse than football, no worse than basketball. I believe it's the public that makes the sport as brutal as it is. David slew Goliath. Look at Samson. Look at Moses and the Hebrew boys. All those guys were warriors.

Marvis Frazier

British Heavyweights

Mexicans are always tough with lots of heart; Koreans raw and gritty; the poor British tend to stand up straight and take it on the chops, bleeding almost before the opening bell.

Stephen Brount

On Bruce Woodcock – Sleep came as it must come to all British heavyweights, midway in the fifth round.

'Red' Smith

Don Cockell is the biggest thing on canvas since 'The Wreck of the Hesperus'.

Anon (1955)

Billy Wells was all chin from the waist up.

Frank Moran

In pro boxing, let's face it, the name of the game is how much you make – not how many honours won. Billy Walker was the most successful flop in history.

Reg Gutteridge

On why Henry Cooper quit his greengrocer's business – His potatoes kept getting cut eyes.
Reg Gutteridge

After knocking out his British opponent – They told me Jack Bodell was awkward and he was ... he fell awkwardly.
Jerry Quarry

Richard Dunn's not overawed by this Muhammad Ali. Why, we've got far too many of those black chat merchants back home in Bradford. He's right used to seeing them dance up and down Westgate with their tambourines every Saturday.
Jimmy Devanney

After the press accused him of not trying against Muhammad Ali –
Joe Bugner: Get me Jesus Christ and I'll fight him tomorrow!
Hugh McIlvanney:
Joe, you're only saying that because you know he's got bad hands.

In his prime, Joe Bugner had the physique of a Greek statue but he had fewer moves.
Hugh McIlvanney (1986)

Jesus Christ, 60 per cent of all the Aussies think Joe Bugner is something you find up the Queensland Premier's nose.
***New Australasian Express* (1987)**

Frank Bruno says I'm chicken. Well you can tell him I've come home to roost.
Joe Bugner (1988)

Joe Bugner fought Bruno like the objective of boxing was to get hit on the jaw.
Jim Jacobs (1988)

By the way Frank Bruno went on about beating Bugner, you'd have thought he had won the Booker prize, not just taken time to out-jab an old man bullocking around pretty harmlessly in the pension queue.
Frank Keating *The Guardian* (1988)

Frank Bruno's fall was that of a felled oak. As the dust settled there was a silence, and then followed the gentle rustle of falling leaves of greenbacks.
Frank Keating *Punch*

Bruno still sounds like another British heavyweight, reminding us of Dorothy Parker's line: 'If all the British heavyweights were laid end to end, we wouldn't be surprised.'
***Ring* magazine**

Before the first Tyson fight – Frank Bruno figures to be the biggest British disaster since the Titanic. Las Vegas will bet you even money Bruno doesn't last the first round. He's 7–1 to lose, 6–1 to get knocked out, he's probably 7–5 to get killed.
Jim Murray *Los Angeles Times* (1989)

After winning the world title at the fourth attempt – Frank, you deserve a knighthood, or maybe even Lord of the Rings.
Desmond Lynam *Sportsnight* BBC TV (1995)

On winning the world title – It was like a Michael Jackson concert, Pavarotti, Vera Lynn and VE-Day, all rolled into one.
Frank Bruno *Sportsnight* **BBC TV (1995)**

If Bruno insists on calling himself a world champion, then he is champion only of that portion of the globe not inhabited by any number of superior heavyweights including Riddick Bowe, Mike Tyson, Evander Holyfield, Lennox Lewis, Bruce Seldon, George Foreman, Luciano Pavarotti, Keith Chegwin, Mr Eric Younghusband, 22 Bramble Lane, Stoke Poges …
Robert Philip *Daily Telegraph* **(1995)**

To newly-crowned Frank Bruno – After all the years of punishment you've taken, you must be thinking about giving up pantomime.
Clive Anderson *Clive Anderson Talks Back* **Channel 4 TV (1995)**

Before the Tyson rematch – Frank Bruno has a chin of such pure Waterford crystal, it gives rise to the old adage that people who live in glass jaws shouldn't throw punches. The biggest danger in fighting Bruno is that you might get hit by flying glass.
Jim Murray *Los Angeles Times* **(1996)**

On taking up rugby league after his defeat by Lennox Lewis – In boxing, it's one against one, whereas in rugby league you have 13 guys coming at you, all trying to do you damage. Mind you, my last fight was a bit like that.
Gary Mason (1992)

After Lennox Lewis lost his world title to Oliver McCall – Lennox Lewis has two chances of getting a rematch with McCall – no chance and slim. And slim has just left town.
Don King (1994)

After Lennox Lewis had beaten Tommy Morrison – 'He's the new Ali!' claims boxing guru Manny Steward … seasoned observers wonder if he's talking about Ali Bongo!
Total Sport **(1995)**

Bums Rush

Boxing is built on bums. How else are you gonna know good from bad? How else is a good boy gonna get on top and get experience unless he fights bums? I tell ya, there's a shortage of bums.
Al Braverman (1975)

After another loss by Chango Cruz – The bum was up and down so many times I thought he was an Otis elevator.
Harry Kabakoff (1977)

On looking for a better class of opponent – I don't want to fight no Mexican roadsweepers no more.
Nigel Benn

On being told his next opponent, Chuck Wepner, was another great white hope – That's the only hope he's got.
Muhammad Ali

Gerry Cooney can't fight to keep warm.
Irving Rudd

Years ago we had the Raging Bull, Jake LaMotta. Today, we've got the Raging Bullshit, Bruce Strauss.
Teddy Brenner

On Mike Tyson's '89 second' opponent in his comeback fight – Peter McNeeley, the Great White Hopeless.
***Boston Globe* (1995)**

On the same fight – Peter McNeeley dived in with overarm shots like a child hurriedly learning the doggie paddle in the deep end.
Frank Keating *The Guardian* (1995)

On Tyson's second comeback opponent – The current version of Buster Mathis [Jr.] boasts not just a Michelin man waist but an *embonpoint* that would give him a better shot at starring in the next Wonderbra poster than winning a boxing title.
Richard Williams *The Guardian* (1995)

Counted Out

Since I've retired, I eat less, weigh less, train less and care less.
Ray Mancini

You always say, 'I'll quit when I start to slide.' Then, one morning, you wake up and you've slid.
Sugar Ray Robinson

Sugar Ray Leonard's retirements last about as long as Elizabeth Taylor's marriages.
Bob Arum (1987)

On boxing comebacks – There are certain things you can't get back, like the elastic in your socks.
Eddie Futch

'Ith time to thtop,' pugilitht Chris Eubank announces he is to quit the ring at 29.
***Total Sport* (1995)**

Die Hard, Too

Hector Camacho's great-dream is to die in his own arms.
Irving Rudd

Playing along with suggestions that his brother George was fighting stiffs – Well, we have been trying to get Elvis. He's been dead long enough.
Ray Foreman

I'm the best heavyweight in Canada and I'll still be the best when I'm dead seven years.
George Chuvalo (1979)

Eublank

Eubank tries to project himself as a deep-thinking and articulate gentleman, but fails miserably.
John Smith (1992)

Chris Eubank arrives in the boxing ring posing and parading like a peacock, so risible that even his opponent and his opponent's corner men have to laugh … a preposterous pugilist.

Michael Herd *Evening Standard* **(1992)**

Look at Eubank's last fight. He came in on this bleedin' great crane. I was hoping and praying the crane broke down, 'cos I'd loved to see them get him out.

Henry Cooper (1995)

Chris Eubank lost his recent comeback fight on points … the main one being that he's a total git.

Nick Hancock *They Think It's All Over* **BBC TV (1995)**

After Chris Eubank's second defeat by Steve Collins – Were you as surprised as we all were when he came from behind and licked you – in the ring?

Caroline Hook *The Mrs Merton Show* **BBC TV (1995)**

After the same defeat – You'd be hard pushed to write an autobiography … you haven't got a title.

Dennis Pennis *The Sunday Show* **BBC TV (1995)**

A re-match with Eubank is not in my plans. I'm not interested in him because he's got nothing I want … except a Harley-Davidson motorbike.

Nigel Benn (1995)

Familiarity Breeds Contest

I fought Sugar [Ray Robinson] so many times that I'm lucky I didn't get diabetes.
Jake LaMotta

Jake LaMotta and I fought six times. We almost got married.
Sugar Ray Robinson

I only have to read Joe Louis' name and my nose starts to bleed again.
Tommy Farr

Feats Of Clay

When it comes to ballyhoo, Muhammad Ali made Barnum and Bailey look like non-starters, and he had the incandescent quality of the real star which would have made him famous, even if his gift was knitting not fighting.
Michael Parkinson

I'd like to borrow Clay's body for 48 hours. There are three guys I'd like to beat up and four women I'd like to make love to.
Jim Murray *Los Angeles Times* **(1964)**

The only trouble with Cassius Clay is that if ever a guy misplayed a role in history it was he … He was going to show that crime didn't pay. Sonny Liston, at that time, would have been the sentimental underdog in a rattlesnake hunt. Cassius took one year to turn Liston into the most popular public favourite since St George. They gave Cassius the part of the marshal in *High Noon* and he wanted

to be the guy in the black hat. He's the kind of guy who would get people rooting against doctors in an epidemic.
Jim Murray (1965)

I got into the ring with Muhammad Ali once and I had him worried for a while. He thought he'd killed me!
Tommy Cooper

Don't watch Ali's gloves, arms or legs when he's fighting. Watch his brains.
José Torres (1970)

On his flamboyant lifestyle – He stings like a bee, but lives like a W.A.S.P.
Eamonn Andrews (1972)

On Ali still fighting at the age of 39 – He now floats like an anchor, stings like a moth.
Ray Gandolfo (1982)

Ali wouldn't have hit Joe Louis on the bum with a handful of rice.
Tommy Farr

He's not only a lousy fighter, he's a bad actor. Louis or Marciano could have whipped him by telephone.
Dan Digilio (1965)

After Ali had been beaten by Joe Frazier in New York – Why should I feel sorry for Ali? He got two and a half-million dollars for being beaten up. Most of us in this city have to pay for the privilege.
Anon boxing fan

I'll beat Floyd Patterson so bad, he'll need a shoehorn to put his hat on.
Muhammad Ali

I'm so fast I could hit you before God gets the news.
Muhammad Ali

Here I predict Sonny Liston's dismemberment,
I'll hit him so hard, he'll forget where October/November went.
Muhammad Ali (1964)

Stewardess: Mr Ali, please fasten your safety belt.
Ali: Superman don't need no safety belt.
Stewardess: Superman don't need no plane either.

Floored Gems

I was once knocked out by a Mexican bantamweight – six of my pals were swinging him around by his heels at the time.

Randall 'Tex' Cobb

On her husband Ron's defeat by Joe Frazier – I'm a realist. You don't enter a Volkswagen at Indy unless you know a helluva shortcut.

Darlene Stander

I've been knocked down more than any heavyweight champion in history, but I consider that a compliment, because I must have got up more than any heavyweight champion.

Floyd Patterson (1972)

When you're knocked down with a good shot, you don't feel pain. In fact it's a very lovable feeling. Maybe it's like taking dope. It's like floating. You feel you love everybody – like a hippie, I guess.
Floyd Patterson (1970)

On Larry Holmes taking on Mike Tyson – We could be wincing witnesses of the worst tumble taken by a Holmes since Conan Doyle put us ringside at the Reichenbach Falls. Sherlock came back after that one. This must be Larry's last stand.
Hugh McIlvanney *The Observer*

After being knocked out – Mike Tyson dropped me. and when I looked up, the count was on five. I said to myself, 'Damn, whatever happened to one to four.'
Buster Mathis Jr (1995)

Glove Story

On being asked, by a female reporter, if he watched his opponent's eyes or gloves – His gloves, dear. I've never been hit by an eye in my life!
Terry Downes

The dumbest question I was ever asked by a sportswriter was whether I hit harder with red or white gloves. As a matter of fact, I hit harder with red.
Frank Crawford

My God, kids today think that the laces are for tying up the gloves.
Fritzie Zivic

Give the average Briton the choice between a warm turn-up with the gloves and the best of gymnastic displays, and he will generally choose the former.
P. G. Wodehouse (1901)

If they cut my bald head open, they will find one big boxing glove. That's all I am.
'Marvellous' Marvin Hagler

I'll bet th' hardest thing 'bout prize fightin' is pickin' up yer teeth with a boxin' glove on.
Francis 'Kin' Hubbard

Hide And Seek

On Billy Conn, who threatened to use his mobility against the world champion – He can run, but he can't hide.
Joe Louis (1941)
[*After his defeat a sportswriter interviewed the elusive Conn and asked:* When did you first know you had a no-hitter?]

Me and Jake LaMotta grew up in the same neighbourhood. You wanna know how popular Jake was? When we played hide and seek, nobody ever looked for LaMotta.
Rocky Graziano

Hitting The High C's

If Mike Tyson gets any better, he'll be hitting Lou Rawls while he sings the National Anthem.
Arsenio Hall (1987)

On Joe Frazier's attempt to sing The Star Spangled Banner *in tune* – I've made the national anthem a six-point underdog.

Jimmy 'The Greek' Snyder

Musically speaking, if Larry Holmes don't C sharp, he'll B flat.

Muhammad Ali

Iron Mike

On the brevity of Mike Tyson's early fights – Mike's like a Gershwin or Beethoven. You go for the quality of the performance, not the longevity of it.

Don King (1989)

Nothing is going to stop Mike Tyson that doesn't have a motor attached.

David Brenner *New York Times* (1988)

Everything Tyson's got has 'goodnight' written on it.

Mills Lane

Tyson fights like you stole something from him or said something nasty about his family.

Mike Acri

After Buster Douglas knocked out Tyson – He's just like Humpty Dumpty. They're not going to be able to put Tyson back together again.

George Foreman (1990)

Mike Tyson's not all that bad. If you dig deep … dig real deep, dig, dig, dig, dig, dig, deep, deep, go all the way to China … I'm sure, you'll find there's a nice guy in there.

George Foreman

On a potential match with Mike Tyson – It would be like the elephants standing up on two feet. It would be like the man being shot out of the cannon. It would be like a woman with a beard down to the floor. It would be the greatest show on earth.

George Foreman (1995)

Mike Tyson has recently found Islam, so his next fight could be a Ramadan-a-Ding-Dong affair.

Rory Bremner (1995)

A rematch with Mike Tyson is as attractive as Sam Fox and Maria Whittaker put together.

Frank Bruno (1995)

When Mike Tyson gets mad, you don't need a referee, you need a priest.

Jim Murray *Los Angeles Times* (1996)

Lawless

I used to nick suits for a living, now I pay a grand for them.

Chris Eubank (1993)

On an FBI investigation into his finances – They went down the list of every known charge conceivable to man: racketeering, skimming, kickback, ticket scalping, fixing fights, pre-ordaining fights, vitiating officials, corrupting judges, all the way down to laundering money. Everything, but the Lindbergh baby.

Don King

Saying that Howard Cosell quit commentating on boxing because it's sleazy is like saying Nixon quit politics because it's crooked.

Paul Gereffi

Since I didn't want to go round mugging old ladies or robbing banks, I took up boxing.

Frank Bruno

Looks Bad

Brain London possesses the most unbeautiful face – it looks as if it, at one time, fell apart and was reassembled by a drunken mechanic.

Michael Parkinson

Terry Downes' face looked as if he had slept on it.

Michael Parkinson

Baroness Summerskill: Mr Cooper, have you looked in the mirror lately and seen the state of your nose?
Henry Cooper: Well, madam, have you

looked in the mirror and seen the state of your nose? Boxing is my excuse. What's yours?

Ingemar Johansson is a leviathan with a strangler's hands and a smile like the beam of a lighthouse.

Louis T. Stanley

Sonny Liston's so ugly, that when he cries the tears run down the back of his head.

Muhammad Ali (1964)

Joe Frazier's so ugly they ought to donate his face to the World Wildlife Fund.

Muhammad Ali (1971)

On his shaven head – With four sisters about the house, I could never get my hands on a comb.

'Marvellous' Marvin Hagler

John Conteh has a neck like a stately home staircase.

Tom Davies

After his gruelling world title fight with Oliver McCall – My head looks like ET gone wrong.

Frank Bruno (1995)

Don King dresses like a pimp and speechifies like a store-front preacher.

John Schulian

Meal Ticket

On monetary demands after winning the world title – Everybody wants a piece of the cake, but my cake has no slices.
Ingemar Johansson

On hitting a shaken opponent – His legs turned to spaghetti and I was all over him like the sauce.
Vinnie Pazienza

If Larry Holmes is the people's champion, then asparagus is the people's vegetable.
Bernie Linicome *Chicago Tribune*

I want to keep fighting because it is the only thing that keeps me out of the hamburger joints. If I don't fight, I'll eat this planet.
George Foreman (1990)

On Evander Holyfield's dietary needs – He's got a nutritionist, and I've got room service.
George Foreman

General Gowon of Nigeria: I used to do some boxing.
Muhammad Ali: What did you box? Apples or oranges?

Media Hype

I'm always into a positive black image. Whenever Leon Spinks fights I always pray, 'Dear Lord, please don't let them interview Leon on TV.'
Arsenio Hall

Boxing is a great exercise ... as long as you can yell 'cut' whenever you want to.
Sylvester Stallone

On a strange offer after becoming world champion – Pose nude for *Playgirl*! I wouldn't pose nude for *Boxing News*.
John Conteh (1974)

Nigel Benn is like washing-up liquid: built on hype and one day the bubble will burst.
Chris Eubank (1990)

Officially Speaking

On choosing a referee for his fight against Floyd Patterson – It don't matter as long as he can count up to ten.
Sonny Liston

Always work the ref's blind side.
Fritzie Zivic

To hell with the Queen of Marksbury.
Pierre Bouchard (1973)

Pain Attention

So many of Barry Hearn's boxers end up in hospital, he should sell his limousine and buy an ambulance.
Mickey Duff

On his prowess as a cut-man – I can close any cut in the world in 50 seconds, so long as it ain't a total beheading.
Adolph Ritacco (1980)

Before fighting Pernell 'Sweet Pea' Whitaker – When I get done with 'Sweet Pea', he'll be 'Split Pea'.
Greg Haugen

On Naseem Hamed – He just wants to get in there and mash them. If you broke his arm, he'd kick you. If you broke his leg, he'd bite you. If you took out his teeth, he'd nut you. This boy wants to fight.
Brendan Ingle (1995)

Pique Fitness

Naseem Hamed is naturally fit. I've seen more fat on a butcher's apron.
Reg Gutteridge, ITV (1995)

Some people say George Foreman is fit as a fiddle, but I think he looks more like a cello.
Lou Duva (1990)

Plan Of Attack

During a fight against Muhammad Ali – Butch Lewis is making no attempt to get out of the corner … and is hanging his chin out like a lantern in a storm.
Reg Gutteridge (1972)

There seems only one way to beat George Foreman: shell him for three days and then send the infantry in.
Hugh McIlvanney (1974)

On Muhammad Ali's rope-a-dope tactics against Foreman – Ali fought over the ropes as if he was leaning backwards out of the bathroom window to see if the cat was on the roof.
George Plimpton (1974)

On Vinnie Pazienza fighting Greg Haugen – Because this is a title fight, I can have four people in the corner and I'll have an extra cut-man. I'll also have an extra stool, one for Vinnie to sit on, and the other to throw at him if he doesn't listen to me.
Lou Duva (1987)

Floyd Patterson is everything a world heavyweight champion should be – except busy.
Rocky Marciano

Price Fighters

I'd love to fight Gerry Cooney. But I have my price – 25 cents and a loose woman.
Randall 'Tex' Cobb

They're selling video cassettes of the Ali–Spinks re-match for $89.95. Hell, for that money Leon will come to your house.
Dr Ferdie Pacheco

Not being born to parents who were accountants was probably my biggest mistake.
Chris Eubank (1995)

I came from a dirt farm, now I'm filthy rich.
Larry Holmes

Don King doesn't care about black or white. He just cares about green.

Larry Holmes

The Inland Revenue Service is the real undefeated heavyweight champion. They show you the left. You never see the right. They'll take everything, even your tears.

George Foreman (1974)

Putting an ex-fighter in the business world is like putting silk stockings on a pig.

Jack Hurley (1981)

On measuring punches in terms of prize money – Jack Dempsey hit me hardest, 'cos Dempsey hit me 211,000 dollars' worth, while Joe Louis only hit me 36,000 dollars' worth.

Jack Sharkey

Punching Power

Jack Dempsey hits like an epileptic pile-driver.

Harry C. Witwert

On taking a punch to the head – It opens a spacious firmament to the bewildered eyes, wherein you discover more planets in a second than most distinguished astronomers observe in a lifetime.

Professor Ned Donnelly *Self-Defence, or The Art of Boxing* (1897)

On being hit by Joe Louis – It's like someone jammed an electric light bulb in your face, and busted it. I thought half my head was blowed off ... When he knocked me down I could have stayed there for three weeks.

James J. Braddock

Rocky Marciano didn't know enough boxing to know what a feint was. He never tried to out-guess you. He just kept trying to knock your brains out.

Archie Moore

Before his fight with Cassius Clay – I can be found the next couple of months trying to perfect my new punch – the lipbuttoner.

Archie Moore

On his fight with Floyd Patterson being switched to the Windy City – Don't matter where the fight is. My punches are just as hard in Chicago as in New York.

Sonny Liston

On knocking out Jimmy Ellis – When I hit Jimmy with that left it felt like when you hit a baseball and it goes right into deep field.

Joe Frazier (1970)

Muhammad Ali isn't a puncher. He just hit me so many times I didn't know where I was.

Brian London

George Chuvalo's best punch is a left cheek to the right glove.

Larry Merchant

George Foreman can knock down an oak tree, but oak trees don't move.
Angelo Dundee (1974)

After knocking out Michael Moorer – Sure the fight was fixed. I fixed it with my right hand.
George Foreman (1994)

On a possible second encounter with Larry Holmes, having been heavily beaten in the first match – I don't think his hands could take the abuse.
Randall 'Tex' Cobb

Larry Holmes doesn't hit as hard as Earnie Shavers. Nobody hits like Shavers. If anybody hit harder than Shavers, I'd shoot him.
Randall 'Tex' Cobb

Earnie Shavers hit me, man, and knocked me face down on the canvas. I was in the land of make believe. I heard saxophones, trombones. I saw little blue rats, and they were all smoking cigars and drinking whisky.
James 'Quick' Tillis

On being asked to name his best punch – I don't know, I've never hit myself.
Elisha Obed

My three best punches were the choke hold, the rabbit punch and the head butt.
Chuck Wepner

On hitting Johnny Bumphus while he was still rising from his stool – The bell went ding and I went dong.
Lloyd Honeyghan

I know it's said that I can't punch, but you should see me putting the cat out at night.
Chris Finnegan

Before fighting Iran Barkley – He's gonna need an industrial-strength toothpick to pick the leather out of his teeth. I'm gonna hit this man so hard he's gonna grow an Afro.
Michael Olajide

Francesco Damiani punches with all the violence and bad intentions of Mahatma Gandhi.
Jerry Izenberg *Newark Star-Ledger*

I get worried when a guy goes down, in case he doesn't get up – for me to hit him again.
Nigel Benn

The right cross-counter is distinctly one of those things which is more blessed to give than to receive.
P. G. Wodehouse *The Pothunters* (1902)

After being stripped of his world light-heavyweight title – I lost it by default, not de-punch.
John Conteh

Rhyme And Punishment

Herol Graham has turned defensive boxing into a poetic art. Trouble is, nobody ever got knocked out by a poem.
Eddie Shaw

If bullshit was poetry, Ray 'Boom Boom' Mancini's name would be Shakespeare.
Dennis Rappaport

For Muhammad Ali to compose a few words of real poetry would be equal to an intellectual throwing a punch.
Norman Mailer

Sponge Men

On managers and promoters – Never in the ring of human conflict have so few taken so much from so many.
Saoul Mamby

A lot of boxing promoters couldn't match the cheeks of their buttocks.
Mickey Duff

Barry Hearn is still a legend in his own mind.
Mickey Duff

Boxing is a great soap opera but at the moment it's *Coronation Street* without balls, and I want it to be *Dallas* with balls.
Barry Hearn (1989)

Bob Arum is one of the worst people in the western hemisphere. I don't know the eastern hemisphere very well, but I suspect he'd be one of the worst people there too, if he went.
Cus D'Amato

Don King is one of the great humanitarians of our time. He has risen above that great term, prejudice. He has screwed everybody he has ever been around. Hog, dog, or frog, it don't matter to Don. If you got a quarter, he wants the first 26 cents.
Randall 'Tex' Cobb

I told Don King that if God needed a PR man he'll send an earthquake or a hurricane along.
George Foreman

Don King's unashamed 'Hi Mom!' camera-hogging makes Fatima Whitbread look like a Carmelite.
Frank Keating

On Don King's award of the keys to the city of Scranton, Philadelphia – Since then we've changed the locks.
Mayor James McNulty

One day Don King will asphyxiate by the force of his own exhaust.
Carmen Graziano (1989)

Before Don King started insulting me I was a complete unknown in this country. Now people stop me and ask for my autograph.
Frank Maloney (1993)

Taking The P!

On being asked for a drug test urine sample immediately after winning a world title – It's marvellous. You win the championship of the world and the first thing they say to you is 'Piss off!'
Jim Watt

On rumours that Oliver McCall failed to provide a drug test urine sample after his defeat by Frank Bruno – Anyone who studied McCall's contribution to the fight would not have been surprised that he failed to hit a sample tube with the required amount afterwards. Bruno, of course, had no such trouble. He is well used to having the piss taken out of him by his fellow countrymen.

Peter Corrigan *Independent on Sunday* **(1995)**

Trouble And Strife

On Mike Tyson's tempestuous marriage to Robin Givens – Whenever he would tell me about their arguments, I begged him, 'Whatever happens, do not hit your wife.'

José Torres (1988)

On Lennox Lewis fighting a five foot nine inch opponent – They say they have picked Justin Fortune because he's the same height as Mike Tyson. So is my wife.

Frank Warren (1995)

Weights And Measures

On his 'overnight excess' after beating Mike Tyson – Buster Douglas went to bed as a 231-pound world champion and woke up as a 270-pound parade float.

Scott Ostler

Anyone who weighs over 200 pounds can punch – I don't care if it's a broad.
Angelo Dundee

They call Ray Robinson the best fighter, pound for pound. I'm the best fighter, ounce for ounce.
Willie Pep

I was six foot one inch when I started fighting, but with all the uppercuts I'm up to six foot five inches.
Chuck Wepner

World Ranking

Las Vegas is the oasis of outstretched palms.
Reg Gutteridge

I don't mind the title fight going out at three in the morning. Everyone in Glasgow fights at three in the morning.
Jim Watt (1980)

In Willie DeWit, we have an all-American boy, even though he is a Canadian.
Billy Joe Fox

On promoting a fight in South America – Venezuela! Great, that's the Italian city with the guys in the boats, right?
Murad Muhammad (1992)

Answering the fight doctor during his title bout against José Torres – You're damn right I know where I am! I'm in Madison Square Garden getting the sh*t kicked out of me.
Willie Pastrano

RAY LINDWALL HAS NOW FINISHED HIS OVER, GOES OVER TO THE UMPIRE, TAKES HIS SWEATER AND STRIDES OFF.
Rex Alston, BBC Radio

Bat To The Future

I don't like defensive shots, you can only get threes.
W. G. Grace

To those who insist on asking who was the greatest batsman, Trumper or Bradman, I feel the only fitting answer is another question: which was the finer seaman, Sinbad the Sailor or Popeye the Sailorman?
Raymond Robinson *From the Boundary* (1951)

Sir Donald Bradman
Would have been a very glad man
If his Test average had been .06 more
Than 99.94.
T. N. E. Smith

I never wanted to make a hundred. Who wants to make a hundred anyway? When I first went in, my immediate objective was to hit the ball to each of the four corners of the field. After that, I tried not to be repetitive.
Lord Learie Constantine

In the first World Cup final - Clive Lloyd hits him high away over mid-wicket for four, a stroke of a man knocking a thistle top with a walking stick.
John Arlott (1975)

On facing the England 'pace' attack – I'd like to paint my face black and go in for the West Indies against our bloody attack.
Geoff Boycott (1981)

To David Gower – If I could add your shots to my brain, I would be an incredible player.
Geoffrey Boycott

Telegram message to Geoff Boycott after he had taken an age to score 50 at Perth – You have done for Australian cricket what the Boston Strangler did for door-to-door salesmen.
Jack Birney

Geoff Boycott has the uncanny knack of being where fast bowlers aren't.
Tony Greig

Now this next question has absolutely nothing to do with either music or sport … At which ground did Geoffrey Boycott hit his hundredth hundred?
Heard on Classic FM (1992)

I can't really say I'm batting badly. I'm not batting long enough to be batting badly.
Greg Chappell

Bonny Botham, my oh me
Hit the ball at ten to three
Didn't come down 'til after tea.
Jeff Cloves

On a savagely hit Ian Botham boundary – None but the brave deserves the four.
John Arlott (1978)

Ian Botham plays a net as if he is on Weston-super-Mare beach and the tide is coming in fast.
Frank Keating

Botham? I could have bowled him out with a cabbage, with the outside leaves still on.
Cec Pepper

It was Jung, I think, who said we learned from our failures, success merely confirming us in our mistakes. What can I learn from my batting failures at Test level?
Mike Brearley (1981)

One is always a little nervous when watching England bat.
Peter May (1984)

To Brian Lara – I don't suppose I can call you a lucky bleeder when you've got 347.
Angus Fraser (1994)

On the Kent batsman giving Lancashire's Ian Austin the charge – Matthew Fleming used to be in the Green Jackets, but the way he's batting suggests he'd be better suited in the Light Brigade.
Charles Colvile, Sky Sports TV (1995)

If the Poms bat first, let's tell the taxi to wait.
Australian fans' banner (1995)

England will win if Camilla Parker bowls.
Australian fans' banner (1995)

Bob-Tail Enders

I don't mind bowling out the rabbits, but that bugger had myxomatosis.
Anon

If I could bowl at myself, I would be very keen. It would be an amputation job to get the ball out of my hand.
Kevin Jarvis (1985)

On South Africa's spinning prodigy Paul Adams coming in to bat at number 11 – A waste of five minutes.
Geoff Boycott, BBC Radio (1995)

Body Line

On the West Indies' bouncer controversy – This is a Test match. It's not Old Reptonians versus Lymeswold; one off the mark and a jolly good show.
David Gower (1984)

In future, I shall always be able to tell when the cricket season begins. All I have to do is listen to the sound of Brian Close being hit by a cricket ball.
Eric Morecambe (1976)

Drop Shots

After the Rev. David Sheppard had dropped a catch off his bowling – You might keep your eyes shut when your praying, Vicar, but I wish you'd keep 'em open when I'm bowling.
Fred Trueman (1963)

On the saboteurs who dug up the Headingley Test wicket – I'd throw them off the top of the pavilion. Mind you, I'm a fair man, I'd give them a 50–50 chance. I'd have Keith Fletcher underneath trying to catch them.
Fred Trueman (1975)

There is nothing in cricket more calculated to raise a laugh than the sight of some determined and serious man under a spiralling catch.
Peter Roebuck *Tangled up in White* (1990)

Chunnel Vision

A pair: a batsman dismissed for a duck in each innings. From the phrase used in French cricket *une au-pair* – literally 'a woman'.
Tim Brooke-Taylor *Cricket Box* (1986)

Alan Knott is small, pokey, alert as a cat … as alive to possibilities of misadventure as a boy playing French cricket on a bumpy lawn.
John Thicknesse

Close To The Edge

Billy Ibadulla had more edges than a broken pisspot.
Fred Trueman

A snick by Jack Hobbs is a sort of disturbance of a cosmic orderliness.
Sir Neville Cardus

Committee Decision

On the Jurassic Park *dinosaurs* – I could go to any county committee room if I wanted to see that.
Fred Trueman (1993)

On the England Chairman of Selectors – I have a lot I could say about Illingworth. If I had my way, I would take him to Traitor's Gate and personally hang, draw and quarter him.
Ian Botham (1995)

Definition: vb. to 'illingworth', to meddle, to interfere, to stick one's oar in. 'Illingworth' … probably comes from the term 'shillingworth', all that could be bought for a single shilling. Thus to 'illingworth' implied a miserliness, a reluctance to squander resources.
Dan Glaister *The Guardian* (1995)

Being the manager of a touring team is rather like being in charge of a cemetery – lots of people underneath you, but no one listening.
Wes Hall (1995)

Cover Point Of View

When asked what he thought of the First Test – What are they testing?
George Bernard Shaw

Novelty is the one quality required for Christmas games … If a game is novel it is enough. To the manager of a toy department the continued vogue of cricket must be very bewildering.
A. A. Milne

I have always imagined cricket as a game invented by roughnecks in a moment of idleness by casually throwing an unexploded bomb at one another. The game was observed by some officer with a twisted and ingenious mind who devoted his life to inventing impossible rules for it.

Peter Ustinov

I am to cricket what Dame Sybil Thorndike is to non-ferrous welding.

Frank Muir

I have seen cricket, and I know it isn't true.

Danny Kaye

Creased Lightning

After he had been run out twice in one match – Arthur Booth is a slow bowler, and on the evidence of this match the characteristic would appear to apply equally to his running.

J. M. Kilburn

Denis Compton was the only player to call his partner for a run and wish him good luck at the same time.

John Warr

During a mid-wicket conference in a Test match –
Ken Barrington: Let's cut out some of

the quick singles.
Fred Titmus: OK! We'll cut out yours, Ken.

Cross Selection

Bombshell: the exclusion of a cricketer from a team.
J. B. Morton [Beachcomber]

Leaving out Dennis Lillee against England would be as unthinkable as the Huns dropping Attila.
Anon Australian TV commentator (1982)

It's a marvellous thing to play for England. You get a few quid, it's nice for the family, and you wear three lions on your chest.
Derek Randall

On minor 'changes' made to the England team – If what the selection committee came up with for Trent Bridge is rebuilding, I don't want them doing my renovations.
Ian Chappell *Adelaide Advertiser* (1990)

On the inclusion of a former Australian youth player in the England test team – Martin McCague will go down as the rat who joined a sinking ship.
***Sydney Daily Telegraph-Mirror* (1993)**

On the influence of Keith Fletcher in the England Test team – I can't bat, I can't bowl and I've played for Essex. So I must have a shout for England.
Ray East, aged 46 (1993)

We have a gaping hole in the England side because Ian Botham has gone. People say Chris Lewis will take his place and I always say, 'What, on the bus to the ground?'
Fred Trueman (1993)

A Yorkshire cricketer is one born within the sound of Bill Bowes.
Michael Carey

On the sacking of Viv Richards and Joel Garner – The Somerset County Cricket Club committee is to fair play what Colonel Gaddafi is to air safety.
Jan Foley (1986)

If Mike Gatting had sworn at the barmaid and sh**ged the Pakistan umpire he'd probably be Chairman of Selectors now.
Nick Hancock *They Think It's All Over* BBC TV (1995)

Doggerel

Cricketer: a creature very nearly as stupid as a dog.
Bernard Levin *The Times* (1965)

This bowler's like my dog: three short legs and balls that swing each way.
Brian Johnston

Taking a cricket ball away from Clarrie Grimmett during a match was like taking a bone from a dog.
R. S. Whitington

Dress Code

The traditional dress of the Australian cricketer is the baggy green cap on the head and the chip on the shoulder. Both are ritualistically assumed.

Simon Barnes *The Times*

Sunday League cricket: multi-coloured pyjamas, two-tone umpires, and white balls with black seams. There is nothing like traditional English sport.

David Hunn *The Sunday Times (1992)*

On the English women's World Cup win – The days of women's cricket being seen as a knicker parade must be over.

Norma Izard (1993)

Some women think that because they play a masculine game they have to look masculine. Some women associated with women's cricket are only ever seen in chunky sweaters and slacks. I get to the stage where I feel embarrassed with some of them. After all it doesn't take much of an effort to buy a pair of shoes with heels on.

Rachel Heyhoe-Flint (1970)

Fan To See Cricket

Watching cricket is easy. All anyone needs is a deckchair, a pipe or knitting, and a week off from the office.

Time **magazine**

Watching cricket is habit forming, it can become habitual,
It's a kind of long-lasting white-robed ritual.
And until recently it's been a male prerogative,
Played by big hairy bowlers and blacksmiths who were slogative.

Gavin Ewart

It's a funny kind of month, October. For the keen cricket fan it's when you realise your wife left you in May.

Denis Norden

On Michael Angelow's £20 bet during the England–West Indies Test at Lord's – ... and a freaker, we've got a freaker down the wicket now. Not very shapely, and it's masculine.

John Arlott, BBC Radio 3 (1973)

English crowds are like sherry. West Indian crowds are like rum. Australian crowds are like Foster's.

Peter Roebuck *Tangled up in White* **(1990)**

Female Grace

It is easier to choose a bat than pick a wife. A bat has a watermark of quality – the grain. The one basic flaw in the otherwise perfect constitution of women is that you can't detect the knots in the grain until it is too late.

Michael Parkinson *Bats in the Pavilion* **(1977)**

You should treat women the same way as any good Yorkshire batsman used to treat a cricket ball. Don't stroke 'em, don't tickle 'em, just give 'em a ruddy good belt.
Fred Trueman

In women's cricket, there's been an uproar recently, because they've had the Bodyform series – where they're actually aiming at the box.
Lee Hurst *They Think It's All Over* BBC TV (1995)

In response – They're not called that in women's cricket – it's a manhole cover.
David Gower *Ibid*

On a female streaker – I thought they were only allowed two bouncers in one over.
Bill Frindall, BBC Radio 4 (1995)

Food And Drink

Sign outside his butcher's shop in Sydney – I used to bowl tripe, then I wrote it, now I sell it.
Arthur Mailey

I see that Northamptonshire have a new bowler called Kettle. May I suggest to Keith Andrew that the best time to put him on would be ten minutes before the tea interval.
Letter to *The Cricketer* (1959)

On traditional cricket teas – We used to eat so many salads, there was a danger of contracting myxomatosis.
Ray East

On the Mike Gatting 'barmaid in hotel room' affair – I don't believe the stories, because I know that nothing goes into Gatt's room after 10.30 p.m. unless he can eat it.
Ian Botham

Despite advertising the cereal on TV – I wouldn't eat Shredded Wheat. I don't like sawdust with milk all over it.
Ian Botham (1990)

You're regarded as a soft guy in Holland if you play cricket. They think it's all eating lunch and tea, and pretty boring.
Andre van Troost (1993)

How to cure a cricketer's red nose – drink till it's purple.
J.B. Morton [Beachcomber] *Daily Express*

Drink is a serious problem, particularly on cricket tours, for it can be said, without fear of contradiction, that nothing yet devised by man is worse for a sick hangover than a day's cricket in the summer sun.
Michael Parkinson *Bats in the Pavilion* (1977)

Football

If my mother hadn't thrown my football boots on the fire, I might have become as famous as Denis Compton.
Sir Len Hutton

On the reverse sweep – It's like Manchester United getting a penalty and Bryan Robson taking it with his head.
David Lloyd (1987)

God Free Heavens

Geoff Boycott's idea of bliss might be to bat all night, having batted all day.

John Woodcock

A cricket tour in Australia would be the most delightful period in one's life, if one was deaf.

Harold Larwood

Oh God! If there be cricket in heaven let there also be rain.

Alec Douglas-Home

When I get to heaven I shall produce on my behalf, in hope of salvation, my stock of failures and frustrations. My attempt to become a leader writer on the *Manchester Guardian*, my attempts to sing the *Abscheid of Wotan*, my attempts to understand Hegel, my attempts to spin a fast ball from the leg to the off stump.

Neville Cardus

Grounds And Pitches

The wicket reminded me of a middle-aged gentleman's head of hair when the middle-aged gentleman, to conceal the baldness of his crown, applies a pair of wet brushes to some favourite long locks and brushes them across the top of his head.

Fred Gale (1868)

He played his cricket on the heath,
The pitch was full of bumps.
A fast ball hit him on the teeth,
The dentist drew the stumps.
Anon

The Oval, Canterbury, Brighton and Fenner's always produced good wickets; but Lord's was terribly bad, and it was said that the only respect in which the pitch resembled a billiard table was the pockets.

Harry Altham *A History of Cricket* (1926)

You know Lord's? Well, once I played
there
and a ball I hit to leg –
Struck the umpire's head, stayed there
As a nest retains an egg.
Harry Graham Ruthless Rhymes

On the suggestion that Test pitches had been deliberately prepared to suit England – It is the prerogative of the home country to prepare the type of pitch they want. We will play them in the car park if that is what they want.
Wes Hall (1995)

Pitches are like wives, you can never tell how they're going to turn out.
Sir Len Hutton (1954)

Headline News

After England's defeat in Holland –
CLOGGED!
The Sun (1989)

After England's defeat by India –
BOMBAY POTATOES
The Sun (1993)

After England's defeat by Sri Lanka –
A LOAD OF LANKAS
The Sun (1993)

Helmets

There was a young fresher called Gilbert Jessop
Who was pitching it less up and less up.
Till one of the pros,
Got a blow on the nose,
And said 'Inside a helmet I'll dress up'.
Anon Cambridge student

England's pace bowlers are making the helmet go out of fashion.
Scyld Berry

Illness And Injury

Is it possible that the current outbreak of chicken-pox affecting the England cricket tourists could be caused by the incessant shouting of Mike Gatting to 'Catch it!'?
John Banfield, letter to *Daily Telegraph* (1994)

Yorkshire were 232 all out. Sir Len Hutton ill ... No! I'm sorry, Hutton 111.
John Snagge, BBC Radio

After the New Zealand batsman was dealt a painful blow to the box by the fifth delivery of an over – Glenn Turner looks a bit shaky and unsteady, but I think he's going to bat on – one ball left.
Brian Johnston

I've had about ten operations. I'm a bit like a battered old Escort. You might find one panel left that's original.
Ian Botham (1993)

Infieldels

The fieldsmen are scattered in the wilderness like missionaries.
John Arlott

Seeing Trevor Bailey prepare for a session in the field was like a lecture in anatomy.
Ray East

Keeping Up Appearances

Dr W.G. Grace,
Had hair all over his face.
Lord! How all the people cheered,
When a ball got lost in his beard.
E. C. Bentley

Colin Milburn is as untidy as an unmade bed, as devastating as a hand grenade.
Clive Taylor

John Jameson is expressionless and big. Big in the way they used to describe barrel chested; which means that he looks as if he is permanently holding his breath.
Clive Taylor

If you imagine Clive Lloyd as being small, white, and right-handed, then you've got Gilbert Jessop.
Anon

Richard Hadlee has the appearance of a rickety church steeple and a severe manner which suggests that women are not likely to be ordained yet.

Peter Roebuck *The Cricketer*

To the moustachioed Dennis Lillee – Are you aware, Sir, that the last time I saw anything like that on a top lip, the whole herd had to be destroyed.

Eric Morecambe

Lillee is wearing a voluminous nightshirt which would have room for another man, if he could get into the trousers.

John Arlott

Alan Butcher drops his head, both hands behind his back and looks sheepishly down the wicket like a small boy caught stealing jam.

John Arlott

On Asif Masood's bowling action – He approaches the wicket like Groucho Marx chasing after a pretty waitress.

John Arlott

It's difficult to be more laid back than David Gower without being actually comatose.

Frances Edmonds

The words 'laid back' fit as snugly around Gower's blond curls as a halo.

Peter Hayter

On the South Africans' penchant for facial sunblock – What bemuses me is why they should come out after dinner in a day–night match facially smeared like Hottentots seeking missionaries served medium rare.

Ian Wooldridge *Daily Mail* (1996)

Cricket is the only game that you can actually put on weight when playing.

Tommy Docherty

During the 1985 India v England Test in Calcutta –
David Gower: Do you want Gatting a foot wider?
Chris Cowdrey: No. He'd burst.

Legs XI

Neil Harvey's at slip, with his legs wide apart, waiting for a tickle.

Brian Johnston

Fred Titmus has two short legs, one of them square.

Brian Johnston

L.E.G. Ames
Was good at games
But when batting at cricket
He was always L.E.G. before wicket.

James Moss

Professional coaching is a man trying to get you to keep your legs together when other men have spent a lifetime trying to get them apart.

Rachel Heyhoe-Flint

After the ball which Raman Subba Row had dropped off Fred Trueman's bowling had gone for four –
Subba Row: I'm sorry about that, it might have been better if I had kept

my legs together.
Trueman: Aye, it's a pity your mother didn't!

Limited Overs

On the early days of Sunday League cricket – For six days, thou shalt push up and down the line, but on the seventh day thou shalt swipe.
Doug Padgett (1969)

On one-day cricket – The dot ball has become the Holy Grail.
Colin Cowdrey

During the 1975 World Cup final – They've scored off the last 15 balls – now difficult not only to bowl a maiden over, but apparently a maiden delivery.
John Arlott

One-day cricket is like fast food. No one wants to cook.
Viv Richards (1988)

In one-day games batsmen are as homogeneous as baked beans.
Peter Roebuck *The Sunday Times* **(1985)**

Inner rings are splendid for those within them.
Peter Roebuck *Tangled up in White* **(1990)**

Media Hype

And when you rub the ball on rump or belly,
Remember what it looks like on the telly.
A. P. Herbert

Suggested title for his autobiography – The definitive volume on the finest bloody fast bowler that ever drew breath.
Fred Trueman

Music

It would be extremely difficult for me to choose between singing Elvis Presley songs and scoring a century for England, but I think I would choose a century for England.
Tim Rice (1981)

Chris Lewis is the enigma with no variation.
Vic Marks (1994)

Officially Speaking

At her first game of cricket – What are the butchers for?
Pauline Chase

It is rather suitable for umpires to dress like dentists, since one of their tasks is to draw stumps.
John Arlott

I cannot for the life of me see why the umpires, the only two people on a cricket field who are not going to get grass stains on their knees, are the only two people allowed to wear dark trousers.
Katherine Whitehorn

Umpire Harold Bird, having a wonderful time, signalling everything in the world, including stopping traffic coming on from behind.
John Arlott

If there were an Olympic event for running backwards, I would be the obvious favourite.
Harold 'Dickie' Bird *Not Out* **(1978)**

My only complaint with 'Dickie' Bird is that he requires a degree of certainty that is almost neurotic; like the man who has to keep going to the front door to make certain that he's locked it.
Mike Brearley

There should have been a last line of defence during the war. It would have been made up entirely of the most officious breed of cricket stewards. If Hitler had tried to invade these shores he would have been met by a short, stout man in a white coat who would have said, 'I don't care who you are, you're not coming in here unless you are a member!'
Ray East (1983)

Old Tossers

As harrowing occupations go, there can't be much to choose between the Australian cricket captaincy and social work on Skid Row.
Doug Ibbotson

There's only one head bigger than Tony Greig's and that's Birkenhead.
Fred Trueman

The statistics suggest that Mike Brearley is one of the great England captains. The luckiest would be nearer the truth.
Ray Illingworth (1980)

On a meddling non-captain – Phil Edmonds needs two more field changes to get his 1,000 for the season.
Jim Laker

After going 4–0 down in the Ashes series – Mr Gower is the most disastrous leader since Ethelred the Unready. Beyond question he should now stand down in favour of Ken Dodd.
The Sun **(1990)**

Pace In Out Time

Fast bowlers are a breed apart, and Fred Trueman was apart from the breed.
Denis Compton

Tell me Fred [Trueman], have you ever bowled a ball which merely went straight?
Richard Hutton

They said to me at the Oval, come and see our new bowling machine. 'Bowling machine?' I said, '*I* used to be the bowling machine.'
Alec Bedser

On facing the 'quicks' – To have some idea what it's like, stand in the outside lane of a motorway, get your mate to drive his car at you at 95 mph and wait until he's 12 yards away before you decide which way to jump.
Geoff Boycott (1989)

Norman Cowans should remember what happened to Graham Dilley, who started off as a genuinely quick bowler. Then, they started stuffing line and length into his ear, and now he has Dennis Lillee's action with Denis Thatcher's pace.
Geoff Boycott (1982)

They should cut Joel Garner off at the knees to make him bowl at a normal height.
Geoff Boycott

Michael Holding is a perfect running specimen, but I don't go to a Test to see running; if I wish to see that I would go to Crystal Palace to see Coe and Ovett.
Jack Fingleton

To dismiss this lad, Mike Denness, you don't have to bowl fast, you just have to run up fast.
Brian Close (1974)

Ashes to ashes, dust to dust –
If Thomson don't get ya, Lillee must.
Sydney Telegraph (1975)

Telling dear old Devon Malcolm to bowl down the corridor of uncertainty is like asking bombers to demolish a city without hurting any civilians.
Peter Roebuck *The Sunday Times* (1993)

Devon Malcolm is the scattergun of Test cricket, capable on his worst days of putting the fear of God into short leg and second slip rather than the batsman. But sometimes, when the force is with him and he puts his contact lenses in the correct eyes, he can be devastating.
Mike Selvey *The Guardian* (1995)

Paradise Lost

If you're going to lose, you might as well lose good and proper and try to sneak a win.
Ted Dexter

On Graham Gooch receiving the OBE, after losing the Ashes series – It must stand for 'Overwhelmingly Beaten Englishman'.
Ian Chadband (1991)

On England's defeat by Holland on a matted wicket – We didn't read the mat conditions at all.
Keith Fletcher (1993)

Rebel Yell

On World Series Cricket – Kerry Packer's Flying Circus.
Tony Lewis (1979)

I am not my brother's wicket-keeper.
Clyde Packer (1977)

On the unofficial England tour to South Africa – The ANC should now admit that it had its tactics wrong all along. Nelson Mandela, instead of pointlessly getting himself locked up for life, merely because he wanted his people to be free, should have concentrated on his batting skills.
Phillip Cole, letter to *The Guardian* (1989)

Spinsters

On his figures of 4 for 362 from 64 overs, when Victoria scored a record 1,107 runs – If that chap in the brown derby hat at the back of the grandstand had held his catches, I'd have had them out days ago ... Very few chances were given, but I think a chap in a tweed coat dropped Jack Ryder near the shilling stand ... It was rather a pity that Ellis got out at 1,107, because I was just striking a length.

Arthur Mailey (1926)

Clarrie Grimmett thought a full toss was the worst form of cricket vandalism and the long hop a legacy from pre-historic days when barbarians rolled boulders towards the enemy.

Arthur Mailey

On South African spinner 'Tufty' Mann continually outfoxing England batsman George Mann – So what we are watching here is a clear case of Mann's inhumanity to Mann.

John Arlott (1948)

On Jim Laker's ten wickets in a Test innings – No bugger ever got all ten when I was bowling at the other end.

Sydney Barnes (1956)

Bill O'Reilly's googly was harder to spot than a soda fountain in the bush.

Colin McCool

At Grace Road, Leicester – You've come over at a very appropriate time; Ray Illingworth has just relieved himself at the pavilion end.

Brian Johnston

A Yorkshire team without a left-arm slow bowler would be like an army without its general, a jockey without a horse, a fish without chips.

Don Mosey

When you're an off-spinner there's not much point glaring at a batsman. If I glared at Viv Richards he'd just hit me even further.

David Acfield (1982)

Shane Warne is the raider of the lost art.

Bob Holmes *The Observer* **(1994)**

On how to play Shane Warne – My tactic would be to take a quick single and observe him from the other end.

Geoff Boycott (1994)

I forget it's Shane Warne and just think of him as any old bowler lobbing down a lump of leather.

Brian Lara (1995)

My wife had an uncle who could never walk down the nave of an abbey without wondering whether it would take spin.

Alec Douglas-Home *The Twentieth Century Revisited* **(1982)**

If the good Lord had ever shown me how to pick out the googly from a leg-break at a range of about 20 yards I would not now be a sportswriter.

Ian Wooldridge *Daily Mail* **(1979)**

Sportsmanship

The only time an Australian walks is when his car runs out of petrol.

Barry Richards (1980)

After Trevor Chappell's underhand delivery prevented New Zealand from winning a limited overs game – Australians Have An Underarm Problem.

New Zealand banner

The synthetic indignation of certain English cricketers over alleged Pakistani ball-tampering: the unedifying in pursuit of the unbeatable.

Patrick Collins *Mail on Sunday* (1992)

On the Mike Atherton ball-tampering row – Athers to Athers, dust to dust.

Sign outside a pub in Reading, Berkshire (1994)

Stage And Sightscreen

A Test match without Ian Botham is like a horror film without Boris Karloff.

Fred Trueman (1989)

On Botham's Christmas pantomime performance – The only thing more wooden on the stage was the tree.

Anon (1994)

Reviewing a stage adaptation of Henry Fielding's Tom Jones – Good Fielding. No Hit.

Kyle Crichton

Sub-Incontinent

On being asked what he looked forward to most upon returning from a long tour of India – A dry fart!

Phil Edmonds

Pakistan is the sort of place every man should send his mother-in-law to, for a month, all expenses paid.

Ian Botham (1984)

On suffering from diarrhoea on tour in India – I just want to get into the middle and get the right sort of runs.

Robin Smith (1993)

During England's tour of India – I've done the elephant. I've done the poverty. I might as well go home.

Phil Tufnell (1993)

Un-American Activities

England and America should scrap cricket and baseball and come up with a new game that they both can play. Like baseball, for example.

Robert Benchley

A cricket bat is an instrument that looks like a baseball bat run over by a steamroller.

Anon

Cricket is baseball on valium.

Robin Williams

Cricket is a tough and terrible rough unscrupulous game. No wonder our American friends do not like it.

A. P. Herbert in a speech at Surrey County Cricket Club dinner

Village Cricket

Villagers do not think village cricket is funny.

John Arlott (1981)

The mere mention of the words 'village' and 'cricket' conjures up a sepia-toned rustic idyll, full of burly blacksmiths and wily off-spinning parsons and chaps called Jack with pipes, who always score a hundred in even time but never hit across the line.

Marcus Berkmann *Rain Men* (1995)

Winning Or Losing

I want to play cricket, it doesn't seem to matter if you win or lose.
Meat Loaf

On limited-over cricket – Sixteen needed from two overs. If we win, jubilation; if we lose, despair. It matters not how we played the game, but whether we won or lost.
Vic Marks (1988)

After England lost the Ashes 4–0 – Mickey Stewart said the England players do not think about defeat. Some of them do not seem to think about much at all.
Mike Selvey *The Guardian* (1990)

After the West Indies record one-day defeat by Australia – We're not really batting ... from the captain to the cook.
Richie Richardson (1995)

NEVER GO FOR A 50–50 BALL UNLESS YOU'RE 80–20 SURE OF WINNING IT.

Ian Darke, Sky Sports TV

Can-Cantona

After signing the Frenchman at Leeds United – Eric Cantona gave interviews on art, philosophy and politics. A natural room-mate for David Batty, I thought immediately.

Howard Wilkinson *Managing to Succeed* (1992)

After Cantona's kung-fu kick on a Crystal Palace supporter – The Sh*t Hits The Fan!

***Daily Star* headline (1995)**
(*N.B.* The Sun *ran a picture caption* – The Twit Hits The Fan!)

On the same incident – It's really a case of him losing les marbles.

Gary Lineker (1995)

On the same incident – I would have cut off his testicles.

Brian Clough (1995)

On Cantona's subsequent lengthy FA ban – I don't think anyone in the history of football will get the sentence Eric got ... unless they had killed Bert Millichip's dog.

Alex Ferguson (1995)

After Cantona's arrest for the above incident – Ooh, Aah, Prisonaa!

***The Sun* headline (1995)**

(Comedienne Jo Brand 'claimed' to have heard West Ham supporters chanting: 'Ooh, Aah, French W**ka!')

The final comment from a legal expert with his finger firmly on the pulse, albeit a weak one – What I don't understand is how a Frenchman can be playing for Manchester United. He's not even from England. They employ him to play football for them, not to go round hitting people.
Lord Denning QC (1995)

Chairman Of The Bored

After being told to 'Start performing, or else!' by Birmingham City owner David Sullivan – We could do without comments like that, especially from someone who doesn't know a goal-line from a clothes line.
Barry Fry (1994)

My chairman at Aston Villa, Doug Ellis, said he was right behind me, so I told him I'd rather have him in front of me where I could see him.
Tommy Docherty

On Alan Sugar's allegations about a 'bung' – The second he's brave enough, big enough, gets a bloody shave and doesn't walk like a spiv, then I'll sue him if he repeats it.
Brian Clough (1995)

We now live in an age of the high-profile chairman. He wants power, glory, prestige. He even wants to run the game. Yet these are the people who took us into the Inter Two-Bob Cup.
Jimmy Greaves (1995)

On learning that Chelsea fans wanted Matthew Harding to replace him as club chairman – So what? Ninety-nine per cent of all Iraqis voted for Saddam Hussein.
Ken Bates (1995)

Cross Selection

Before Nottingham Forest's 1990 Littlewoods Cup Final – The only person certain of boarding the coach for the Final is Albert Kershaw, and he'll be driving it.
Brian Clough

After the player-manager dropped himself from a losing Shrewsbury team, which then won – Perhaps I found our weakness at last.
Graham Turner (1980)

Some of the people who have been picked for England recently should have written back to the FA saying 'There must be some mistake, I can't play.'
Raich Carter (1981)

When I joined Rangers I immediately established myself as third-choice left-half. The guys ahead of me were an amputee and a Catholic.
Craig Brown

I have seen things on *Star Trek: The Next Generation* that I find easier to believe than the fact that Mike Duxbury was once an England regular.
Nick Hancock *Total Sport* (1995)

Defensive Markings

If there is an effective way of killing off the threat of Diego Maradona by marking him, it probably involves putting a white cross over his heart and tethering him to a stake in front of a firing squad. Even then, there would be the fear that he might suddenly drop his shoulder and cause the riflemen to start shooting one another.
Hugh McIlvanney *The Observer* (1986)

It's easy to beat Brazil. You just stop them getting 20 yards from your goal.
Bobby Charlton (1970)

On how to mark Ruud Gullit – If all else fails, you could wait for the first corner and tie his dreadlocks to the goalpost.
Vinnie Jones

Defenders Of The Realm

On QPR's Alan MacDonald marking Wimbledon's John Fashanu – He was a dedicated follower of Fashanu.
David Lacey *The Guardian* (1993)

On Arsenal's delayed flight from Copenhagen – When the captain said there was a problem at the back, I thought he meant me and Steve Bould.
Tony Adams (1994)

I never went in for aerial challenges at Liverpool. You lose 150 brain cells every time you head a ball; I used to make Mark Lawrenson do all the heading. You have to delegate. It's a captain's prerogative.
Alan Hansen (1993)

On Manchester United's captain Martin Buchan accepting the FA Cup at Wembley – How appropriate that there should be 39 steps for Buchan to climb to receive the Cup.
John Motson, BBC TV (1977)

Gary Mabbutt: Dodgy defender who's often caught in two minds. Abbott and Costello's.
***Zit* (1993)**

To find a way past Bobby Moore was like searching for the exit from Hampton Court maze.
David Miller *The Times* (1993)

On his goal in the 1967 European Cup Final against Inter Milan – As I came to shoot, a defender stopped and half-turned his back on me. If he'd taken another step it would have been very difficult for me to get the ball past him. They say the book of Italian heroes is very thin and he wasn't into expanding it any.
Tommy Gemmell (1985)

People talk about Julian's haircut and his tackling and how aggressive he looks but I don't see him like that. I could see him in a tutu and ballet shoes. He is a big girl's blouse.

Mrs Kay Dicks (1995)

Dressed To Skill

It is left feet that are usually called educated; David Beckham's right probably has an MA.

Ian Ridley *Independent on Sunday* **(1995)**

Should Gheorghe Hagi become just a fraction more clinical in slicing open the opposition, he may have to play the rest of the World Cup in a mask and gown.

Hugh McIlvanney *The Sunday Times* **(1994)**

When Geoff Thomas traps the ball it goes as far as I used to be able to kick it.

George Best (1993)

A million quid for Mark Hateley? But he can't even trap a dead rat.

Stan Bowles

With Scott Nisbet every pass is an adventure.

Walter Smith (1993)

Fan To See Football

On Rochdale's postponed FA Cup game against Manchester United – We were very disappointed we couldn't play on Saturday, because like United, we had supporters coming from all over the country. There were two coming from London, one from Newcastle, one from Brighton and …

David Kilpatrick (1986)

Support means getting behind the team through thick and thin. Newcastle fans have, in the last few years, been through thin and thin.

Kevin Keegan (1992)

At Newcastle the crowd is worth one and a half goals' start to the home side, but here at Southend it's probably minus six.

Vic Jobson (1992)

In Glasgow half the fans hate you and the other half think they own you.

Tommy Burns (1987)

On English hooligans abroad – They deserve to be flogged and made to break rocks for five years – with their heads.

Daily Star (1993)

We do have the greatest fans in the world, but I've never seen a fan score a goal.

Jock Stein (1982)

Watching a football match without bias is like watching *Neighbours* without a lobotomy – very boring.

Marius Brill *The Sunday Times* **(1994)**

After Ipswich's game against Spurs, their first following a 9–0 defeat by Manchester United – Three-nil, we only lost three-nil.

Ipswich fans' chant (1995)

Fast Forward

The trouble with Earl Barrett is that he's one-paced – Zoooomm!

Joe Royle (1990)

They called Steve Kindon the 'Horse' because of his speed. It was also because he had the brain of a clothes horse and the control of a rocking horse.

Paul Fletcher

Football is like a car. You've got five gears and the trouble with England teams is that they drive all the time in fourth or fifth.

Ruud Gullit (1995)

Freak Kicks

Facing a Ronald Koeman free kick is like facing a serial killer

Archie MacPherson (1992)

It's being rumoured that Man. Utd are trying to sign Michel Platini, just in case they get a free kick on the edge of the box this season.

Mike Ticher *When Saturday Comes* **(1986)**

Full Members Cup

West Ham Debate What They Can Do To Change Dicks.

***The Times* headline**

Footballers are only interested in drinks, clothes, and the size of their willies.

Karren Brady (1993)

Gaffers And Guvnors

When you get to a certain age, there is no coming back. I've decided to pick my moment to quit very carefully – in about 200 years time.

Brian Clough (1991)

On his eventual retirement – Like all great dictators from De Gaulle to Thatcher, Brian Clough stayed on a little too long.

***Gazzetta dello Sport* (1993)**

On West Brom fans' post-match protests – That's not the worst reception I've ever had, did you ever see me as a player?

Bobby Gould (1992)

Tommy Docherty: the human Scotweiler.

Anon

On Tommy Docherty – Who would have guessed that behind that arrogant Scots bastard image there lay an arrogant Scots bastard?

Mike Ticher *When Saturday Comes* **(1986)**

When the TV people asked me if I'd like to play a football manager in a play, I asked how long it would take. They told me 'About ten days', and I said, 'That's about par for the course.'

Tommy Docherty (1989)

If, as every Englishman suspects, the Scots ingest a weakness for hyperbole with their mother's milk, Ally MacLeod would seem to have been breast-fed until he was 15.

Hugh McIlvanney *The Observer* **(1978)**

I think Ally MacLeod believes tactics are a new kind of peppermint.

Anon Scottish World Cup international (1978)

Bobby Robson's natural expression is that of a man who fears he might have left the gas on.

David Lacey *The Guardian*

Bill Shankly – the man who put the 'er back into soccer.

Mike Ticher *When Saturday Comes* **(1986)**

They call him Big Ron Atkinson because he is a Big Spender in the transfer market. I just call him Fat Ron.

Malcolm Allison (1993)

On becoming manager at Southend – I must admit when I came here I thought we were certs to finish bottom. Now I am very optimistic and I think we'll finish second bottom.

Barry Fry (1993)

Before being sacked, by Ken Bates, as Chelsea manager – Compared to the chairman I had at Southend, Ken Bates is Mary Poppins.

David Webb (1993)

Who wants to be a football manager? Well, people like me who are too old to play, too poor to be a director and too much in love with the game to be an agent.

Steve Coppell (1993)

After George Graham had been sacked by Arsenal – Out On His Arsenal.

Daily Star **headline (1995)**

Q. What is the difference between George Graham and British tennis players?
A. George Graham can return backhanders.

The Onion Bag **(1995)**

His answerphone message – I am not here at the moment. If you are the president of AC Milan, Barcelona or Real Madrid I will get back to you.

Joe Kinnear (1995)

Gay Meadow

On Justin Fashanu joining Airdrie (nicknamed the Diamonds) – Queen of Diamonds.

The Sun **headline (1993)**

Elton John decided to rename Watford, he wanted to call it Queen of the South.

Tommy Docherty

My relationship with Kenny Dalglish did not get off to the best of starts mainly due to the fact he thought I was a poof.
Graeme Souness *No Half Measures* **(1985)**

Globall

On receiving the freedom of Nottingham – It's a beautiful city with lovely people. The Trent is lovely, too. I know, I've walked on it for 18 years.
Brian Clough (1993)

On Scotland's game in San Marino – We've been playing for an hour and it's just occurred to me that we're drawing 0-0 with a mountain top.
Ian Archer, BBC Radio Scotland (1991)

If we had rugby union's ten-metre rule in our game, Willie Miller of Aberdeen would have played most of his football in Norway.
Tony Higgins (1991)

On reports that Brazilian Juninho would find the north-east too cold – It's not exactly the North Pole. Maybe we should be getting him a snow plough instead of a club car.
Bryan Robson (1995)

Governing Bodies

A merger between the FA and Football League would be like putting two dinosaurs together and getting a dodo.
Gordon Taylor (1991)

The Football League is run by small men with even smaller minds. They have shown the impartiality, wisdom and far-sightedness of a committee of Pakistani [cricket] umpires.

Robert Maxwell

Football hooligans? Well, there are the 92 club chairmen for a start.

Brian Clough

The English First Division – the new, hyperbolic status for the erstwhile Second Division. This is a world of hard men and fluffed chances – park football writ large … The First Division is a greasy cheeseburger dressed up as an alfresco meat dish.

Tony Parsons *The Observer Magazine* **(1992)**

On the Football Association – Everyone knows that a few clubs and some promotions men are now running the new Premier League. The organisation with the unfortunate initials seems to be doing, well, putting it politely, not much.

Norman Fox *Independent on Sunday* **(1992)**

Grid Irony

The rules of soccer are very simple, basically it is this: if if moves, kick it. If it doesn't move, kick it until it does.

Phil Woosnam (1974)

The rest of the world loves soccer. Surely we must be missing something. Uh, isn't that what the Russians told us about communism? There's a good reason why you don't care about soccer – it's because you are an American and hating soccer is more American than mom's apple pie, driving a pick-up and spending Saturday afternoon channel-surfing with the remote control.

Tom Weir *USA Today*

On England's 2–0 defeat by the USA in Boston – The biggest English disaster since losing India ... the biggest win for the USA since we beat the mighty Trinidad and Tobago.

Bob Ryan *Boston Globe* (1993)

On the same game – Blimey! US boots the Brits.

Boston Herald (1993)

On Pele's legacy in the USA – People smoked Pele, drank Pele coladas, and vacationed in the Pele Islands, but for us he never became anything more than that little guy from down there somewhere who could bounce a ball on his head.

Dan Jenkins *Playboy* (1985)

Hair Pieces

Footballers today have haircuts resembling a hedge, Gazza's intellect and know the words of *The Birdie Song*.

Noel Sweeney (1991)

On Paul Gascoigne's changing hair colour – What happens if he has an off dye?

Peter Corrigan *Independent on Sunday* (1995)

Denis Law, the Lawman, so-called because his second name was Law and he was a man. It was he who had the reactions of a mongoose, and the hairstyle as well.

It's Only an Excuse (1986)

How much further down his head will Bobby Charlton have to part his hair before he faces the fact that he is bald?

Clive James

Ruud Gullit has everything apart from a short-back-and-sides.

John Toshack (1988)

Roberto Baggio's a great footballer, but what an egregious haircut. It takes the damage Ian Botham inflicted on follicular sculpture a few frightening steps further. It's out beyond even the highlights zone ... Would you walk down the street with someone with a semi-quiff, no sideburns and a ponytail halfway up the back of his head?

Andrew Anthony *For Him Magazine* (1992)

Alexei Lalas looks like the love child of Rasputin and Phyllis Diller

Sports Illustrated (1994)

Have It Away Games

It seems Charlie Nicholas is getting a lot of everything except for the ball.
Jimmy Greaves (1984)

I've always believed in treating the ball like a woman. Give it a cuddle, caress it a wee bit, take your time, and you'll get the required response.
Jim Baxter (1991)

First love, second football. Maybe photo finish.
Giamperiero Masieri

After scoring for Hungary in the 1952 Olympic final – I got so many kisses after this goal, they would probably have sufficed a modest woman for a lifetime.
Ferenc Puskas

People always say I shouldn't be burning the candle at both ends. Maybe because they don't have a big enough candle.
George Best

If you'd given me the choice of beating four men and smashing in a goal from 30 yards against Liverpool or going to bed with Miss World, it would have been a difficult choice. Luckily I had both. It's just that you do one of those things in front of 50,000 people.
George Best (1991)

I always had a reputation for going missing – Miss England, Miss United Kingdom, Miss World ...
George Best (1992)

If I had the choice of a night with Raquel Welch or going to the betting shop, I'd choose the betting shop.
Stan Bowles

If Stan Bowles could pass a betting shop like he can pass a ball he'd have no worries at all.
Ernie Tagg

Watching Channel 4's *Love Weekend* was all a bit much. You began to hanker for something love-free, like an Arnold Schwarzenegger film, or a Division Two football match.
Marcus Berkmann *Daily Mail* **(1993)**

Height And Weight

Following the recent freak storms in south-east England, many of London's finest trees have been destroyed or damaged. The condition of Niall Quinn was later said to be satisfactory.
When Saturday Comes **(1987)**

After playing against six foot seven inch Kevin Francis – He was quite daunting. If I ever need any guttering fixed, I'll give him a call.
Ray Wilkins (1994)

Jan Molby looked corpulent enough to be playing darts for Denmark.
Brian Glanville *The Sunday Times* **(1985)**

When the team trooped on, Molby looked like a fat man who had tagged on to the Liverpool line to live out every overweight's dream.
Brough Scott *Independent on Sunday* **(1992)**

Waddling around like a recently impregnated hippopotamus ... Paul Gascoigne had become a bona fide wobble-bottom ... But should football finally fail him, at least there's a whole range of alternative careers now on the horizon. Father Christmas ... barrage balloon ... spacehopper ...

Marcus Berkmann *Independent on Sunday* **(1993)**

I've been told that I retain a lot of moisture when I eat.

Paul Gascoigne (1993)

I don't mind what you call me as long as you don't call me late for lunch.

William 'Fatty' Foulkes (1901)

Home, Sweet Home

Since Walsall's new ground is to be built on the site of an old sewage works, may I suggest the new name of W.C. Fields?

Letter to *Birmingham Sports Argus* **(1989)**

Hampden Park is the fourth worst international stadium in the world, just behind those of Latvia, the Solomon Islands and Gibraltar.

The Final Hurdle **(1991)**

Hampden Park is the only ground which looks the same in black and white as it does in colour.

David Lacey *The Guardian* **(1987)**

On joining AC Milan – Blimey! The ground looks a bit different to Watford. Where's the dog track?

Luther Blissett (1983)

White Hart Lane is a great place. The only thing wrong is the seats face the pitch.

Les Dawson (1991)

During a floodlight failure at Upton Park – If you all clap, perhaps many hands will make light work.

Tannoy announcer (1983)

Irish Question

If you have a fortnight's holiday in Dublin you qualify for an Eire cap.

Mike England (1986)

On the news that his striker Stan Collymore was eligible to play for Ireland – I'd be delighted because our transfer agreement with Southend is that we only pay them more if he plays for England.

Frank Clark (1994)

Keepers' Bawl!

Maybe Napoleon was wrong when he said we were a nation of shopkeepers ... Today England looked like a nation of goalkeepers.

Tom Stoppard *Professional Foul* **(1977)**

Dutch goalkeepers are protected to a ridiculous extent. The only time they are in danger of physical contact is when they go into a red light district.

Brian Clough (1985)

If Pat Jennings had been available on that memorable occasion when the Romans met the Etruscans, Horatius surely would have had to be satisfied with a seat on the substitute's bench.

Eric Todd

To add to West Ham's anxiety, Ludek Miklosko, their tree trunk of a goalkeeper, is displaying symptoms of Czech elm disease.

David Lacey *The Guardian* **(1991)**

On Gordon Banks' late replacement in the 1970 World Cup quarter-final – With his yellow shirt and spindly legs Peter Bonetti looked like an accountant on a beach holiday, who'd just wandered on to the pitch … Gordon Banks with food poisoning would have still done better.

Nick Hancock *Total Sport* **(1995)**

After the Colombian's scorpion goal-line clearance at Wembley – It is understood that René Higuita wants to join Arsenal … because they are used to publicity about kickbacks.

Martin Thorpe *The Guardian* **(1995)**

Dino Zoff's all right on the high stuff, but with the low stuff he's been going down in instalments.

Ian St John, ITV (1982)

The Crystal Palace keeper's let in more than the West German government.

Jimmy Greaves (1989)

It took Wales 44 minutes to test Taffarel [in Brazil's goal] and the examination was of the 11-plus variety.

Joe Lovejoy *Independent*

Andy Murdoch [Partick Thistle] has an answerphone installed on his six-yard line, and the message says: 'Sorry I'm not in just now, but if you'd like to leave the ball in the back of the net I'll get back to you as soon as I can.'

Jim Duffy (1991)

Kick It!

I think football would become an even better game if someone could invent a ball that kicks back.

Eric Morecambe

Joe Jordan kicks the parts other beers cannot reach.

Graffiti

After his Birmingham side had missed all four penalty kicks in a shoot-out against Liverpool – At least we were consistent.

Barry Fry (1995)

Learning Curve

I was potentially quite bright at school, but when they'd be telling me about the reproduction of the spyrogyra, all I was thinking was how to get a left back to overlap.
Malcolm Macdonald (1976)

In response to Emlyn Hughes and Mike Channon's World Cup comments on ITV – Conjugate the verb 'done great': I done great, he done great, we done great, they done great, the boy Lineker done great.
Letter to *The Guardian* **(1986)**

Long Ball

If God had meant football to be played in the air, He'd have put grass in the sky.
Brian Clough (1992)

Football wasn't meant to be run by two linesmen and air traffic control.
Tommy Docherty

Balloon ball. The percentage game, Route One … It's crept into the First Division. We get asked to lend youngsters to these teams. We won't do it. They come back with bad habits, big legs and good eyesight.
Ron Atkinson (1984)

Replying to Terry Venables' comment that Graham Taylor's long-ball tactics would put the game back ten years – If Watford could put the game back ten years it would be in a better state than it is now.
Danny Blanchflower (1982)

On Sheffield Wednesday playing Watford, a clash of two long-ball teams – Graham Taylor and myself are going to pump nitrogen into the ball to make it go higher. Then we are going to give it a sedative at 2.30 p.m., an aspirin at half-time and paracetamol at quarter to five. After the match we are going to put the ball in a van and take it to a home provided by the National Society for the Prevention of Cruelty to Football.
Howard Wilkinson (1984)

On Graham Taylor's long-ball tactics as England manager – As a vision of the future it ranks right up there with the SDP and the Sinclair C5.
Joe Lovejoy *Independent* **(1992)**

On Graham Taylor's return to basic tactics – Hump it, bump it, whack it! It might be a recipe for a good sex life, but it won't win the World Cup.
Ken Bates (1993)

Luck & Superstition

On Norwich's bad run of form – With our luck one of my players must be bonking a witch.
Ken Brown (1987)

On Dundee United's travel arrangements – I won't say I'm superstitious about rituals but you should see the route we take when we go to Edinburgh.
Jim McLean (1992)

I don't have lucky signs except my teeth. Sometimes I play with them in and sometimes out.
Martin Chivers (1972)

Marrow Doner

On a positive drug test in World Cup 94 – Don't cry for Maradona, Argentina.
Roddy Forsyth *Sunday Telegraph* (1994)

On the same positive drugs test – Maragoner!
New York Daily News

Midfielders

Billy Bremner: ten stone of barbed wire.
***The Sunday Times* (1970)**

Trevor Brooking floats like a butterfly and stings like one too.
Brian Clough (1981)

Roy Race the fictional Melchester Rovers heroic cardboard cut-out still has more personality than Trevor Brooking.
***Zit* (1993)**

Glenn Hoddle: Tame, cultured ball wizard who thought tackle was something you put in your fishing bag.
***Zit* (1993)**

After Oldham had been knocked out the FA Cup by Spurs – Ossie Ardiles was the difference. It was like trying to tackle dust.
Joe Royle (1988)

I once said Gazza's IQ was less than his shirt number and he asked me, 'What's an IQ?'
George Best (1993)

When I arrived at Liverpool I was at my peak and an England international. Now I'm a Pontins League player.
Nigel Clough (1995)

Money For Old Europe

After John Major's post-leadership election Cabinet reshuffle – I heard that the Foreign Secretary's job had gone to Graham Taylor on the basis that if anyone could get us out of Europe he could.
Sir Ivan Lawrence (1995)

On his successful first season as Barcelona manager – When I arrived in the summer, one of my predecessors told the Spanish media that Mister Terry would be gone by Christmas. He forgot to say which year.
Terry Venables (1984)

In countries such as Spain and Italy, football is considered almost an art form. In this country, it's more Van den Hauwe than Van Gogh.
Gary Lineker *The Observer* (1995)

After his transfer from Aston Villa to Bari in Italy – Someone asked me last week if I missed the Villa. I said 'No, I live in one.'
David Platt (1991)

On the problems Wrexham faced in the Cup-Winners Cup – We went to Oporto and there's a bloody hurricane. We come to Rome and the shops are shut. When we play in the Soviet Union, Ronald Reagan will have probably blown the place up.
Jim Steel (1984)

On Partick Thistle's European Inter-Toto Cup run – The last time Thistle were in Europe the stewardess didn't come round with earphones ... she came round with goggles.
John Lambie (1995)

On leaving Barnet to manage Southend – Everybody wants to take on the best and I do too. I want to pit my wits against all of them: Manchester United, Real Madrid, Juventus and Fray Bentos.
Barry Fry (1993)

I shouldn't have been upset at losing to Benfica. After all, they have the best players, the best referees and the best linesmen.
Jimmy Hagan, Vitoria Setubal manager (1980)

After Manchester United's violent game against Valencia – It's the first time, after a match, that we've had to replace divots in the players.
Ron Atkinson (1982)

I see Atletico Madrid just sacked another manager before the season has even started. He must have had a bad photocall.
Ron Atkinson (1990)

Players in Greece can earn far more selling games than winning them. Everything has a price. You don't need coaches in Greece, you need cashiers.
Joe Mallett (1975)

The Greek squad to face Neasden in the second leg of the Inter-Suburbs European Nations Cup was named in Athens yesterday. It reads: Xenophon, Eggandchippolatas, Aristophanes, Menopaus, Owa'alotigotides, Kikiminthebolox, Logarithm, Thucydides, Chrystalpallas, Delicatessen, Underneaththearches.
Private Eye **(1971)**

Without contact with Europe, English football's dominant characteristics are liable to turn monstrous. A few years and who knows what mutants it will produce. I see Vinniana Jones and the Temple of Doom. I see Creatures the World Forgot.
Robert Pryce *The Guardian* (1989)

Catenaccio: A word used by Brian Glanville to demonstrate his knowledge of Italian football. Its meaning can be loosely translated as 'bribery'.
When Saturday Comes **(1986)**

The last time a team in Scotland lived up to the fans' expectations was in 1960 when Real Madrid beat Eintracht in Glasgow [in the European Cup Final].
Andy Roxburgh (1986)

Moving On

On his reasons for leaving Coventry City – I've been racing Formula One in a Mini Metro.

Bobby Gould (1993)

On being appointed manager at West Brom – My eldest son is playing in goal for Halifax reserves – and I think I've got pressure.

Bobby Gould (1991)

On Paul Gascoigne joining Lazio – I'm pleased for him, but it's like watching your mother-in-law drive off a cliff in your new car.

Terry Venables (1992)

On Torquay's new manager – We made Ivan Golac an offer he should have refused.

Mike Bateson (1992)

On leaving Preston – I left as I arrived: fired with enthusiasm.

John McGrath (1991)

On his brief spell at Leeds United in 1974 – I shouldn't have gone. I thought I could go there and win the European Cup. As things turned out, I'm not sure we ever won the toss.

Brian Clough (1991)

I had 11 clubs – 12 if you count Stringfellows.

Frank Worthington (1993)

On rumours of the Celtic player joining their cross-town rivals – Paul McStay for Rangers? Sounds like a fair swap to me.

Letter to *Sunday Mail* (1992)

On transfer-listed Marcus Gayle – Well, the Salvation Army rang me up. They want him to sell copies of the *War Cry* in the pub on a Sunday afternnon.

David Webb *Middlesex Chronicle* (1994)

Music

Playing with Rodney Marsh is like playing alongside Barbra Streisand.

Mike Summerbee (1973)

On his new signing – How can you put into words what it means having George Best at Dunstable? It'll be a bigger boost for the club than having Frank Sinatra sing at half-time.

Barry Fry (1974)

Lothar Matthäus conducts midfield like a latter day Sir Malcolm Sargent.

Steve Curry *Daily Express*

I met Mick Jagger when I was playing for Oxford United and the Rolling Stones played a concert there. Little did I know that one day he'd be almost as famous as me.

Ron Atkinson (1993)

During the 1992 European Championships – The presence of Manchester City's Paul Lake would have presented England with the all-powerful triumvirate of Merson, Lake and Palmer, which would have been fitting, given that for most of the tournament England displayed about as much subtlety as a bombastic '70s supergroup.
The Absolute Game

Native Tongue

On being linked to the Welsh manager's job – I can't promise to give the team talk in Welsh, but from now on I shall be taking my holidays in Porthcawl and I've a complete set of Harry Secombe records.
Brian Clough (1988)

For the benefit of Anglo-Saxon viewers, I wonder if the TV sports presenters would consider using subtitles when interviewing Kenny Dalglish.
Letter to *Evening Standard* (1986)

The only English I've heard from Eric Cantona is 'Goal!'
Steve Bruce (1993)

Jan Stejskal only knows three words of English: 'My Ball', 'Away' and one other.
Ray Wilkins (1991)

When Dusan Vrto came to Dundee all he could say in English was 'Yes', 'No' and 'Morning'. A week later he'd added 'Thank you' and 'Budweiser'.
Jim Duffy (1993)

On the Brazilian Juninho joining Middlesbrough – He will only need to learn three words: 'Pound', 'Thank You' and 'Bye Bye'.
Jan Aage Fjortoft (1995)

Net Returns

If someone brings me a Martian who can score 25 goals a season, I'll take him. If he only wants £400 a week, even better.
Dave Bassett (1994)

I've had these barren spells. What's the Spanish for that? El blanko runno, I suppose.
Gary Lineker (1987)

Ian Rush's hooter's so big he should have 'Long Vehicle' stencilled on the back of his head.
Danny Baker, BBC Radio 5 (1992)

On the striker's lack of success at Juventus – We know that Ian Rush lets his goals do the talking, but so far he hasn't spoken very much.
Gianni Agnelli, Juventus president (1987)

Tony Hateley had it all. The only thing he lacked was ability.
Tommy Docherty

On Stan Mortensen's death – They'll probably call it the Matthews' funeral.
The Guardian (1991)

Hugo Sanchez is a very dangerous man. He is as welcome as a piranha in a bidet.

Jesus Gil (1992)

During the 1990 World Cup Finals – I've just seen Gary Lineker shake hands with Jürgen Klinsmann – it's a wonder Klinsmann hasn't fallen down.

Ron Atkinson, ITV

Jimmy Greaves used to hang around like a substitute best man at a wedding for 85 minutes and still win more matches than any other player.

Ian Wooldridge *Football Monthly* **(1973)**

Duncan McKenzie is like a beautiful motor car. Six owners and been in the garage most of the time.

John Toshack (1978)

Kenny Dalglish calls all his goals 'tap-ins' until we come to the end of the season and we are talking money. Suddenly he changes his mind.

Bob Paisley (1982)

I'd like to get ten goals this season, but the authorities don't normally let me play for a whole season.

Vinnie Jones (1991)

After Newcastle's Les Ferdinand scored an injury-time equaliser against Chelsea in the FA Cup – Ferd Degree Murder!

***The Sun* headline (1996)**

Officially Speaking

On French referee Joel Quiniou (USA v Brazil) – It's like a toaster, that shirt pocket. Every time there's a tackle, up pops a yellow card.

Kevin Keegan, ITV (1994)

On referees and his reformed disciplinary outlook – I'm doing all right. One booked me the other day, said I was diving. He didn't see the guy kick me from behind. Hopefully, they can overturn that one and I'll only be down to 150 points.

Ian Wright *A Question of Sport* **BBC TV (1995)**

If we painted our footballs orange and threw one to a linesman, he'd probably try to peel it.

Jimmy Gabriel

One Over The Inside Right

They serve a drink in Glasgow called a Souness – one half and you're off.

Tommy Docherty

Alcoholism v Communism.

Scottish World Cup banner v USSR (1982)

Pain Attention

Soccer is to sport what athlete's foot is to injuries.

Tom Weir *USA Today*

On the number of injuries to his US soccer team – I thought about bringing in an acupuncturist from Japan. When I heard how much it cost, I called a dart thrower from Tijuana.

Ron Newman

John Barnes' problem is that he gets injured appearing on *A Question of Sport.*

Tommy Docherty (1993)

For me injuries don't come in threes, they come in 33s.

Paul Gascoigne (1994)

After having his leg amputated – I'll stay in football. I don't mind if they stand me up and use me as a corner flag.

Derek Dooley (1953)

On reports that heading a ball damages brain cells – I don't think heading the ball has got anything to do with it. Footballers are stupid enough, anyway.

Anon Premiership spokesman (1995)

Pint Of Best

Title of his autobiography – 'The Good, the Bad and the Bubbly'.

George Best (1990)

George Best is the drunk we could all have become.

Michael Herd *Evening Standard*

After George Best's comment that 'Kevin Keegan isn't fit to lace my boots' – Keegan isn't fit to lace Best's drinks.

John Roberts

When it comes to majority taste, BBC TV is more out of touch than *Edward Scissorhands* ... The Corporation's light entertainment output currently falls between more stools than George Best.

Garry Bushell *Modern Review* (1994)

Interviewing George Best on her TV show – You were a '60s sensation, and all that marvellous football ... and, of course, all that booze. Did you ever think if you hadn't done all that running around playing football, would you have been so thirsty?

Caroline Hook *The Mrs Merton Show* BBC TV (1995)

Paul Gascoigne is accused of being arrogant, unable to cope with the press, and a boozer. Sounds like he's got a chance to me.

George Best

Playing Kitsch

Next to hooligans the people I'd most like to lose interest in football are kit manufacturers.

Patrick Barclay *The Guardian* (1985)

Modern football shirts look like the work of a chimpanzee on drugs let loose at Brentford Nylons.

Andrew Shields *Time Out* (1994)

Garry Birtles – his weird, way-out gear … the fancy bowties, winged collars and spectacular suits that nobody else would ever wear without the courage of four bottles of wine.

Steve Coppell

Come on you blue two-tone hoops with red and white trim and a little emblem on the sleeve and the manufacturer's logo and the sponsor's name across the chest and …

Mike Ticher *When Saturday Comes* **(1986)**

Over-turning previous manager Peter Withe's 'No Jeans' dress code at Wimbledon – They can wear jeans and earrings for all I care, but I draw the line at stockings and suspenders – until after the match.

Joe Kinnear (1992)

On the 33-year-old joining QPR – Peter Reid's legs looked all right, but the hooped shirt didn't do him any favours.

Howard Kendall (1990)

On why football would not take off in the USA – Reason No 3. Grown men wear short pants outdoors. In America, a man wears short pants outdoors only when he's playing tennis, mowing the lawn or urgently leaving the home of somebody else's wife.

Dan Jenkins *Futbol*

Arsenal FC's away strip – It looks like something you'd reject for the kitchen curtains.

Brian Moore, ITV (1993)

This Spring, Arsenal's goalkeeper David Seaman is wearing a banana-yellow abattoir worker's smock with a fetching inlaid testcard motif, which is attractively repeated in a pair of radioactive side panels on his lycra-style shorts, for that fire-damaged tarpaulin look … Dumb grin, model's own.

Giles Smith *Independent on Sunday* **(1994)**

Political Football

Ossie Ardiles may well be the only Peronist to have played professional football in North London in recent times (excluding Bob Wilson for lack of concrete evidence).

Mike Ticher *When Saturday Comes* **(1986)**

Brazil's football is like their inflation – 100 per cent.

Jornal da Tarde

Maggie isn't the only one with Crooks at No. 11.

Spurs fans' FA Cup final banner (1981)

Pools

Robert Sangster … is a delightful fellow in spite of having £100 million in his current account. It's exciting to think that he wins the pools *every* week.

Jeffrey Bernard *The Spectator*

God moves in a mysterious way
His wonders to perform;
I got eight draws on Saturday
But didn't post the form.
John Davies *When Saturday Comes*
(1987)

The time has come, the Walrus said, to
talk of football pools.
Of fixture lists and copyright, of clever
men and fools.
Percy Rudd *News Chronicle*

Price Is Outside Right

I keep reading that I could earn £400,000
– but to do that Norwich would have to
win the League, the Cup, the Boat Race
and the Grand National.
Mike Walker (1994)

Before Peterborough played
Middlesbrough in the League Cup
quarter-final – I told the players we need
to win so that I can have the cash to buy
some new ones.
Chris Turner (1992)

Scottish football: once a simple game
played by semi-illiterates. Now a multi-
million pound industry played by semi-
illiterates.
It's Only an Excuse **(1993)**

On being sacked by Preston North End
in 1981 – They offered me a handshake
of £10,000 to settle amicably. I told them
they would have to be a lot more
amicable than that.
Tommy Docherty (1983)

On Paolo Rossi's post-World Cup salary
demands – Two months ago he was over
the moon – now he's asking for it.
Anon Juventus executive (1982)

On his money-grabbing players at FC
Cologne – Some of our players can
hardly write their own names, but you
should see them add up.
Karl-Heinz Thielen (1982)

Those were the days that when you
spent seven million quid on Cole, the
chances were you'd just bought South
Wales.
Bob Mills *Soccer Blunderland* **Sky Sports**
TV (1995)

On Dutch striker Marco Boogers – If
players can tie up their bootlaces these
days they seem to be worth one million
pounds. I got one who can't even tie his
laces.
Harry Redknapp (1995)

Religion

Football is like a religion and heaven is a
place on turf.
When Saturday Comes **(1994)**

Trying to gee up Cyrille Regis, his
born-again striker – I know Cyrille's
found God, but now I want him to find
the devil.
Ron Atkinson (1992)

On his becoming a born-again Christian –
I hear Glenn Hoddle has found God. That
must have been one hell of a pass!
Jasper Carrott

David Icke says he's here to save the world. Well, he saved bugger all when he played in goal for Coventry.

Jasper Carrott (1992)

When anybody starts calling me a Messiah, all I have to do is go and see my parents.

Bob Stokoe (1973)

Poster on a Liverpool wall – What would you do if Jesus returned among us?
Graffiti – Move St John to inside left.

Riddles

How many cup-ties would a cup-tie tie if a cup-tie could tie ties?

Frank Keating *Punch*

Ten modern labours of Hercules:
No. 1. Make Kenny Dalglish laugh uncontrollably.

Journolists *Mail on Sunday* **(1990)**

In answer to your question, 'What is always brought to Cup Finals but never used?' (the loser's ribbons that are tied to the cup), the answer should surely be – Malcolm Macdonald!

Laurence Lebor (1978)

Q. Who is the jammiest player in the world?
A. Diego Maradoughnut!

Royalty

Queen In Rumpus At Palace!

***The Guardian* headline concerning Crystal Palace's Gerry Queen (1971)**

Feminists will regret to hear that there was a time in history when the birth of a princess was on a par with defeat in the World Cup.

Arthur Marshall *Sunny Side Up*

Scotch Missed

During the 1978 World Cup Finals – The tune began changing when the Peruvians, one goal down, suddenly revealed an ability to run faster with the ball than the Scots could run without it.

Clive James *The Observer* **(1978)**

On the archetypal Scottish player – He'd have a mixture of Billy Bremner arrogance – small and hard – Kenny Dalglish brilliance, Denis Law, the best-ever goalscorer, Dave Mackay, die-hard, desperate will to win   and he'd have a floppy pair of hands.

Emlyn Hughes (1985)

An enigma is a Scottish euphemism for someone who played a good game and we're all waiting for him to do it again.

***It's Only an Excuse* (1986)**

Seasons To Be Cheerful

It is time enough for football, prosaic and sober
In October ...
Why should the time of mists and mellow fruitfulness
Succumb so soon to this dreary bootfulness?
Paul Jennings

Signings Of The Time

Football is not a game for jokers. If any of my players were to start acting like clowns, I would arrange their transfer to a circus.
Bill Shankly

On Eric Cantona's transfer from Leeds to Manchester United – One minute we're thinking he's an ugly, French, one-eyed git, and then he crosses the Pennines and becomes a dark, brooding, Heathcliff type.
Manchester United fanzine (1993)

Kenny Dalglish can go out and buy the best full-back for Blackburn Rovers but if I talk about buying big, I mean getting someone who is six foot four.
Mike Walker (1993)

On Rangers signing Roman Catholic Mo Johnston – The world of Scottish football was rocked to its pre-cast concrete foundations over the close season when Rangers finally broke with 100 years of tradition and bought a player from FC Nantes for the first time in their history.
The Absolute Game (1989)

On signing Robert Lee from Charlton – He nearly went to Middlesbrough but I told him Newcastle was nearer London. Luckily footballers believe things like that.
Kevin Keegan (1994)

Slogan's Run

Behind every world class goalkeeper there's a ball from Ian Wright.
Nike football boot advert (1993)

This slogan prompted a spoof from across London: Behind every football stadium there's a ball from Tony Adams.
Tottenham fanzine (1993)

In response to an earlier Ian Wright Nike advertising slogan: 'Gary Who?' – Lineker 48, Wright 0.
Quaser boots advertising slogan (1992)
[pointing out the number of England goals each player had scored]

Black Sheep Bitter – slips down easier than Jürgen Klinsmann.
Beer advert (1994)

Earthquakes, wars and Millwall results as they happen.
BBC Radio 5 Live advert (1994)

Welcome to Bologna on Capital Gold, for England versus San Marino with Tennent's Pilsner Lager, brewed with Czechoslovakian yeast for that extra Pilsner taste and England are one down.
Jonathan Pearce, Capital Gold Radio (1993)

On the possibility of sponsoring Stenhousemuir, after using them for a series of adverts – Our company only sponsor the arts. I don't think Stenhousemuir could be regarded by any stretch of the imagination as artistic.
Prudential Insurance PR representative

Song And Dance

I once described football in England as being the working man's ballet. It's more like a clog dance now.
Tony Waddington (1991)

I read in the newspapers that Terry Neill says he'll put the joy back in Tottenham's football. What's he going to do – give them bloody banjos?
Eddie Bailey (1974)

We put bells on a football so Jim Holton would know where it was. We had complaints from morris dancers saying he was kicking them all over the place.
Tommy Docherty

Soccer is a game in which everyone does a lot of running around. Twenty-one guys stand around and one guy does a tap dance with the ball. It's about as exciting as *Tristan and Isolde*.
Jim Murray *Los Angeles Times* (1967)

Skull And Cross Jones

The FA have given me a pat on the back. I've taken violence off the terracing and onto the pitch.
Vinnie Jones in Oxford Union speech (1995)

Vinnie (short for Vindictive) Jones.
***Zit* (1993)**

Hard men? Well, there was that picture of Vinnie Jones holding Gazza's wotsits. In my day we called someone who did that a poof.
George Best (1993)

Vinnie Jones is to fine and fair football what Count Dracula was to blood transfusions.
Michael Herd *Evening Standard* (1992)

Vinnie Jones is as discreet as a scream in a cathedral.
Frank McGhee *The Observer* (1988)

Vinnie Jones is a player who regards it as a matter of personal honour to intimidate the nation's finest, to castrate them with a shattering, late tackle early in the game, to rip their ears off and spit in the hole.
Jasper Rees *Independent on Sunday* (1992)

On his new signing for Sheffield United – I don't expect Vinnie Jones to do Tony Currie things. Currie couldn't do some of the things Vinnie does. When you're building a team, you look for good players, not blokes to marry your daughters.
Dave Bassett (1990)

On his debut for Wales – Stone me! We've had cocaine, bribery and Arsenal scoring two goals at home. But just when you thought there truly were no surprises left in football, Vinnie Jones turns out to be an international player.
Jimmy Greaves *The Sun* (1994)

On his being 90 minutes late for an FA disciplinary meeting – We don't know where Vinnie Jones is. It's puzzling because he knows his way here.

Anon Wimbledon FC executive

Back in my day on the Marshes, Jones wouldn't have got into our Sunday morning team. Ponderous as a carthorse and slow-witted on the field as a football donkey, his bullying would never have compensated for his deficiencies … After all, it is hardly Jones's fault that such a clodhopper – sorry, former hod carrier – has been able to wangle a prosperous living from the professional game.

Jeff Powell *Daily Mail* (1996)

Stinker Taylor ...

Before England's disappointing 0–0 draw with Denmark in Euro '92 – I expect to win. Let me do the worrying, that's what I'm paid for. You get your feet up in front of the telly, get a few beers in, and have a good time.

Graham Taylor (1992)

SWEDES 2 TURNIPS 1

***The Sun* headline June 1992**

SPANISH 1 ONIONS 0

***The Sun* headline September 1992**

After defeat in Norway –
NORSE MANURE

***The Sun* headline June 1993**

After the USA beat England 2–0 in Boston – YANKS 2 PLANKS 0

***The Sun* headline June 1993**

On Graham Taylor after the loss to the USA – THE BOSTON DANGLER

***The Sun* headline June 1993**

After Taylor's England team had finally failed to qualify for the 1994 World Cup – We thought it was all over. It is now.

***Today* headline (1993)**

On Taylor's resignation –
THAT'S YOUR ALLOTMENT

***The Sun* December 1993**

As well as being England's first managerial turnip, Graham Taylor has prime ministerial qualities, combining the personality of John Major with the gift of prophecy of Neville Chamberlain.

Steve Grant *Time Out* (1994)

On The Sun*'s depiction of Graham Taylor as a turnip* – It's a shame they picked on the turnip. The turnip is a wonderful vegetable and it didn't do to do it down. If we were editing *The Sun*, we would choose to compare an England team manager to a lesser-known vegetable such as celeriac, okra or yam.

Jon Meakin of the Fresh Fruit and Vegetable Association, letter to *Evening Standard* (1994)

On the ideal Christmas guest – You may pick Graham Taylor ... he could select your Christmas meal and make all the important decisions, such as who sits where around the table. But you may find that after choosing turkey he suddenly changes his plans at the last minute and decides to have goose instead. Then he'll drop the roast potatoes from the menu, because they're too old. And he's bound to invite Lawrie McMenemy round as well. And John f**king Barnes. So you'll end up with a piss-poor meal and nothing but alcohol-free lager and isotonic Lucozade to drink.

Viz (1994)

Tact Ticks

People keep talking about total football, all I know about is Total petrol.

Derek Dougan

Football tactics are rapidly becoming as complicated as the chemical formula for splitting the atom.

Jimmy Greaves (1963)

Taking Names

I'm particularly unimpressed with the big blond midfielder [Stefan] Effenberg, who has been renamed in our house as Effenuseless.

Peter Corrigan *Independent on Sunday* (1994)

Millichip – v. intrans. to dither, to fail to make up one's mind and eventually to pick the wrong man for a given job. Named from character Sir Bertram Millichip in Dickens' *No Expectations of Winning Anything*.

Private Eye (1994)

Andy Clarke is known as Jigsaw – because he goes to pieces in the box.

Wimbledon match programme

On dying his hair blond for the 1994 World Cup Finals – The boys call me Valderrama but after this game I felt more like Val Doonican.

Andy Townsend (1994)

On football's contemporary glossy image – Players had hearts of oak. They had names of oak, too: Sydney Puddefoot, Jack Cock, Seth Plum and Albert Diaper ... Such names would look foolish in a glossy football magazine. Something with more pizzazz is required: Ginola, Kanchelskis, Cantona, Le Tissier, Yeboah, Aage Fjortoft. Seth Plum wouldn't even have been able to say Aage Fjortoft; he'd have dislocated his jaw trying.

The Men Who Know *The Guardian* (1995)

Teams

Some teams are so negative they could be sponsored by Kodak.

Tommy Docherty

I hear Elton John's made a bid for an Italian club – AC/DC Milan.

Tommy Docherty

Robert Maxwell has just bought Brighton and Hove Albion, and he's furious to find it's only one club.
Tommy Docherty

Chelsea Rule OK.
Whereas Cambridge United exhibit traits indicative of inherent superiority.
Graffiti outside Cambridge United's ground

Hibs 1, Celtic ... they must be getting used to it ... 0.
Sir Alistair Burnett *News at Ten* **ITV (1990)**

Celtic Park has been broken into and the entire contents of the trophy room stolen. Police are believed to be looking for a man with a green carpet.
Anon (1994)

The people in the Everton executive boxes are the lucky ones. They can draw the curtains.
Stan Boardman (1993)

If Everton were playing down at the bottom of my garden, I'd draw the curtains.
Bill Shankly

When I've got nothing better to do, I look *down* the league table to see how Everton are getting along.
Bill Shankly

After Everton had won the 1995 FA Cup – We've laid to rest the 'dogs of war' bit. We're Crufts now.
Joe Royle (1995)

There's only one F in Fulham.
Name of Fulham FC fanzine

Poor Fulham, with no real method up front, resembled a fire engine hurrying to the wrong fire.
Geoffrey Green

This city has two great teams – Liverpool and Liverpool reserves.
Bill Shankly

Yes, we've had hard times at Anfield; one year we came second.
Bob Paisley

The Reds' Prayer:
R Fowler who art in Hansen
Harrower be thy name
Thy Keegan come
Thy Bill be Done
On Byrne as it is in Evans
Lewis this K Hardy Lee bread
And Fagan us our Sounesses
As we Fagan those
Who Souness against us.
And Lidell us Scott
Into Tommo St John
But deliver us from Everton
For thine is the Callaghan
Jack Balmer and Bob Paisley
For Evans and Evans
Our Ken.
***Through the Wind and the Rain* (1994)**

On Manchester City – There are three types of Oxo cubes. Light brown for chicken stock, dark brown for beef stock, and light blue for laughing stock.
Tommy Docherty

Apparently Man City are hoping to exploit fully the Bosman ruling in order to play 11 Germans. That way they can go down with all Hans.

Martin Thorpe *The Guardian* **(1996)**

Nottingham Forest could put ten dustbins out there and do the job they do.

Terry McDermott (1980)

Oldham Athletic? That's a contradiction in terms.

Coronation Street ITV

Life at Oldham is like being a nitroglycerine juggler.

Joe Royle (1994)

Preston are one of my old clubs. So many of them are. I've had more clubs than Jack Nicklaus.

Tommy Docherty (1978)

I promised Rotherham I'd take them out of the Second Division. I did – into the Third Division.

Tommy Docherty *Call the Doc* **(1981)**

If we can sell Newcastle Brown to Japan, if Bob Geldof can have us running round Hyde Park, and if Wimbledon can make it to the First Division, there is surely no achievement beyond our reach.

Margaret Thatcher (1986)

I would rather watch ice hockey than see Wimbledon play. And I hate ice hockey.

John Bond (1991)

After watching Wimbledon – The first half was the sort of thing you'd rather watch on Ceefax.

Gary Lineker (1993)

This elicited the following reply from Dons' manager Joe Kinnear – He's an arsehole, anyway. Not worth two bob, never mind two million.

Wimbledon have as much charm as a broken beer bottle.

Tommy Docherty

Tennis

It's the collective part of the team which is important. If I'd wanted to draw attention to myself I'd have played singles tennis, or chosen a nice lady for mixed doubles.

Eric Cantona (1993)

Replying to Ted Croker's criticism of his club's facilities – I should think the only time he's been to Wimbledon was to see the ladies' final.

Dave Bassett (1986)

After the Dons' shock FA Cup final victory over Liverpool Game, Set and Match to Wimbledon.

Sunday Express headline **(1988)**

On being voted the fifth-best looking sportsman in the world – I was thrilled until I learned Ivan Lendl had finished above me.

Ally McCoist (1990)

Kenny Dalglish has about as much personality as a tennis racket.
Mike Channon

Television And Video

The England football team have released a video called *100 Best Throw-ins*.
Bernard Manning (1993)

Peter Beardsley is the only person who when he appears on television daleks hide behind the sofa.
Nick Hancock They *Think It's All Over* BBC TV (1995)

... The Tough Get Going

This fellow Marco Tardelli, he's likely to leap out the TV at us. He's been responsible for more scar tissue than the surgeons of Harefield hospital.
Jimmy Greaves (1982)

Romeo Benetti – I was at a social function with him the other week, and it's the first time I've got within ten yards of him that he hasn't kicked me. Even then I kept looking over my shoulder.
Kevin Keegan (1978)

Norman Hunter doesn't tackle opponents so much as break them down for resale as scrap.
Julie Welch

The Sugar Plum Fairy could play centre forward if it weren't for people like me.
Peter Storey (1973)

Tommy Smith could start a riot in a graveyard.
Bill Shankly

If Ron 'Chopper' Harris was in a good mood, he'd put iodine on his studs before a game.
Jimmy Greaves

John Fashanu was having karate lessons and ended up a first dan, but he was playing like Desperate Dan.
Joe Kinnear (1993)

David Batty would probably get himself booked playing Handel's *Largo*.
David Lacey *The Guardian* (1992)

After Blackburn team-mates Graeme Le Saux and David Batty came to blows against Spartak Moscow – Before the match I told my players they will be playing against 11 guys ready to fight for each other, not *with* each other.
Oleg Romantsev (1995)

Tradition

Football will always be laddish, no matter how you dress it up. This is a tradition which will never change. At the end of the day, football means not having to go to Asda on Saturday.
The Men Who Know *The Guardian* (1995)

Trouble And Strife

On Denmark's Euro '92 preparations –
I've nothing against letting the wives into
the team camp. Love is good for
footballers as long as it isn't at half-time.

Richard Moller Nielsen (1992)

John Bond has blackened my name with
his insinuations about the private lives of
football managers. Both my wives are
upset.

Malcolm Allison

*On her performance for Arsenal Ladies
in the Women's Cup Final –* I never
expected to get the Man of the Match
award.

Lesley Shipp (1993)

Winger And A Prayer

I'd like to see the return of the wingers –
Matthews and Finney, Hancocks and
Mullen, Huntley and Palmer, and
Fortnum and Mason.

Eric Morecambe (1974)

When Charlie Cooke sold you a dummy,
you had to pay to get back into the
ground.

Jim Baxter

Lee Sharpe has got dynamite in his
shorts.

Stuart Hall, BBC Radio 5 (1993)

You Know, Like

League football in Cambridge is like
having bingo in the Albert Hall.

Anon Cambridge supporter

Carlton Palmer is the worst finisher since
Devon Loch.

Ron Atkinson (1991)

Tommy Docherty criticising Charlie
Nicholas is like Bernard Manning telling
Jimmy Tarbuck to clean up his act.

Gordon Taylor (1984)

That Gheorghe Hagi has got a left foot
like Brian Lara's bat.

Don Howe, ITV (1994)

Comparing Gascoigne to Pele is like
comparing Rolf Harris to Rembrandt.

Rodney Marsh

*On Paul Gascoigne's protective face
mask –* Comparing Gascoigne with the
Phantom of the Opera is to do the
Phantom an injustice – he's playing more
like Sarah Brightman.

**Marcus Berkmann *Independent on
Sunday* (1993)**

Our shot-putters are in better condition
than Gazza.

Linford Christie (1993)

In some respects soccer is a bit like the
dinosaur. You give it a kick up the
backside and three years later its head
drops off.

Ron Jones (1982)

TROUSERS ARE NOW ALLOWED TO BE WORN BY LADIES ON THE COURSE. BUT THEY MUST BE REMOVED BEFORE ENTERING THE CLUBHOUSE.

Sign at an Irish golf club

Advice Precedent

Hit the ball hard and straight and not too often.

Anon

Never bet with anyone you meet on the first tee who has a deep suntan, a one-iron in his bag and squinty eyes.

Dave Marr

Never try to keep more than 300 separate thoughts in your mind during your swing.

Henry Beard *Mulligan's Law* (1994)

Being left-handed is a big advantage. No one knows enough about your swing to mess you up with advice.

Bob Charles (1973)

If you foozle with your cleek,
And your putts are let's say – weak.
If your drives, for all to see,
Do not always leave the tee.
And to slice them is a habit,
If, in short, you're a rabbit.
Do not put your clubs away
Drink a Guinness every day.

An early Guinness advert

The reason the pro tells you to keep your head down is so you can't see him laughing.
Phyllis Diller

Tee the ball high. Because years of experience have shown me that air offers less resistance to dirt.
Jack Nicklaus (1977)

If you drink, don't drive. Don't even putt.
Dean Martin

If you are going to throw a club, it is important to throw it ahead of you, down the fairway, so you don't waste energy going back to pick it up.
Tommy Bolt

On slow play – By the time you get to your ball, if you don't know what to do with it, try another sport.
Julian Boros

Anti-Golf

Golf is cow-pasture pool.
O. K. Bavard

Golf is a good walk spoiled.
Mark Twain

Golf is hockey at the halt.
Arthur Marshall (1985)

On subscribing a shilling to W. G. Grace's testimonial – It's not in support of cricket, but as an earnest protest against golf.
Sir Max Beerbohm

I regard golf as an expensive way of playing marbles.
G. K. Chesterton

Golf is an ineffectual attempt to direct an uncontrollable sphere into an inaccessible hole with instruments ill-adapted to the purpose.
Sir Winston Churchill

If I had my way the social status of professional golfers would be one notch below that of Nazi war criminals.
Andy Lyons *Melody Maker* (1988)

Golf is too slow a game for Canada. We would go to sleep over it
John B. McLenan (1891)

Soccer is a simple-minded game for simple people; golf is merely an expensive way of leaving home.
Michael Parkinson *Bats in the Pavilion* (1977)

There is one thing in this world that is dumber than playing golf. That is watching someone else play golf. What do you actually get to see? Thirty-seven guys in polyester slacks squinting at the sun. Doesn't that set your blood racing?
Peter Andrews

Golf combines two favourite American pastimes: taking long walks and hitting things with sticks.
P. J. O'Rourke *Modern Manners* (1983)

Arnie

Arnold Palmer is the biggest crowd-pleaser since the invention of the portable sanitary facility.
Bob Hope

Palmer lashes into the ball with such explosive force that he almost falls off the tee after his follow through.
Billy Casper (1967)

Being paired with Arnold Palmer is like a two-shot penalty.
John Schlee (1973)

Palmer hitched up his baggy pants and turned golf into a game of 'Hit it hard, go find it and hit it hard again.'
John Schulian

Arnie would go for the flag from the middle of an alligator's back.
Lee Trevino

Arnold Palmer had everything except a brake pedal.
Peter Dobereiner *Golf Digest* **(1982)**

On being asked if his 1966 US Open play-off loss was similar to two previous play-off losses in 1962 and 1963 – Pretty similar ... I lost all three!
Arnold Palmer (1966)

Art Of Golf

Seve [Ballesteros] – the greatest thing to come out of Spain since a painting by Picasso that made sense.
Dan Jenkins

Katsuyoshi Tomori plays golf like Willie Nelson sings. You don't think he can do it but he goes and does it quite well.
Peter Alliss, BBC TV (1995)

Auto-Magic

The difference between learning to play golf and learning to drive a car is that in golf you never hit anything.
Anon

I'm like a 1967 Cadillac. I've changed the engine twice, rolled back the odometer and replaced the transmission. But now all the tyres are going flat, it's time to put it in the junkyard.
Lee Trevino

On trying to sell a Mercedes-Benz prize – It doesn't fit through the Wendy's drive-in.
Scott Hoch

Ball Bearings

Golf is a game in which a ball – one and a half inches in diameter – is placed on a ball – 8,000 miles in diameter. The object being to hit the small ball but not the larger.
John Cunningham

You can't lose an old golf ball.
John Willis *Willis' Rule of Golf* **(1980)**

Golf balls are attracted to water as unerringly as the eye of a middle-aged man to a female bosom.
Michael Green *The Art of Coarse Golf* **(1967)**

Best Years Of Our Drives

When you are too old to chase other things, you can always chase golf balls.

Anon

Any game where a man 60 can beat a man 30 ain't no game.

Burt Shotten

Golf, like the measles, should be caught young, for, if postponed to riper years, the results may be serious.

P. G. Wodehouse *A Mixed Threesome* **(1922)**

Caddie Lacks

There were three things in the world that he held in the smallest esteem – slugs, poets and caddies with hiccups.

P. G. Wodehouse *Rodney Fails to Qualify* **(1924)**

A caddie is someone who accompanies a golfer and didn't see the ball either.

Anon

Real golfers, no matter what the provocation, never strike a caddie with the driver. The sand wedge is far more effective.

Huxtable Pippey

The only time I talk on a golf course is to my caddie. And then only to complain when he gives me the wrong club.

Seve Ballesteros

My game is so bad I gotta hire three caddies – one to walk the left rough, one for the right rough, and one down the middle. And the one in the middle doesn't have to do much.

Dave Hill

On seeing Amy Alcott kissing her caddie after winning the US Women's Open – So that's the secret of winning an Open. First thing Monday I'm gonna fire old Larry and get me a caddie I can smooch.

Lou Graham

If each time a player and caddie split up was actually a divorce, most Tour players would have been 'married' more times than Zsa Zsa and Liz combined.

Peter Jacobsen

On his heavyweight caddie Herman Mitchell – I always know which side a putt will break. It always slopes toward the side of the green Herman's standing.

Lee Trevino

Captain's Plate

I'm not saying my golf game went bad, but if I grew tomatoes they'd come up sliced.

Lee Trevino

Lunch at an American golf course: Club sandwiches, Link sausages, Par-snips, Sliced tomatoes, Tea, Puttatoes.

Anon

The only place Seve Ballesteros turns up for nothing is at his mum's for breakfast.

Howard Clark (1987)

If God had intended a round of golf to take more than three hours, He would not have invented Sunday lunch.

Jimmy Hill

Cart Blanche

*The golf course being rather far
I have an excuse to take the car,
And since the holes are far apart,
I have an excuse to use a cart.
But one thing has me still defeated –
You cannot hit the ball while seated.*

Donna Evleth

You know the old rule: He who have the fastest cart never have to play bad lie.

Mickey Mantle *Esquire* **(1971)**

A golf cart is a two-wheeled bag-carrier that decreases the exercise value of playing 18 holes of golf from about the level of two sets of doubles tennis to the equivalent of an hour and a half of shopping.

Henry Beard *Golfing* **(1985)**

Celebrity Squares

The safest place for spectators in celebrity tournaments is probably on the fairway.

Joe Garagiola (1985)

In the Bob Hope Golf Classic the participation of President Gerald Ford was more than enough to remind you that the nuclear button was at one stage at the disposal of a man who might have either pressed it by mistake or else pressed it deliberately in order to obtain room service.

Clive James *The Observer* **(1981)**

Gerald Ford doesn't realise he can't hit a ball through a tree trunk.

Jack Nicklaus

And the name that is synonymous with Ford – Fore!

Vin Scully (1984)

Gerald Ford – the most dangerous driver since Ben-Hur – has made golf a contact sport. There are 42 golf courses in the Palm Springs area and nobody knows which one Gerald Ford is playing until after he has teed off. It's not hard to find Gerald Ford on a golf course – just follow the wounded.

Bob Hope

Bob Hope says I have made golf a combat and contact sport. But I know I'm getting better at golf because I'm hitting fewer spectators.

Gerald Ford *People* **(1983)**

I would like to deny all allegations by Bob Hope that during my last game of golf, I hit an eagle, a birdie, an elk and a moose.

Gerald Ford

The last time I played with Vice President Spiro Agnew he hit a birdie ... an eagle, a moose, an elk and a mason.

Bob Hope

When I play with Gerald Ford, I usually try to make it a foursome – the president, myself, a paramedic and a faith healer.

Bob Hope

I've done as much for golf as Truman Capote has for Sumo wrestling.

Bob Hope

Sammy Davis Jr hits the ball 130 yards and his jewellery goes 150.

Bob Hope

Jack Benny had only one golf ball the whole of his golfing career. He finally lost it when the string came off.

Bob Hope

Bob Hope has a beautiful short game. Unfortunately, it's off the tee.

Jimmy Demaret

On watching actor Jack Lemmon swing a club – My God, he looks like he's beating a chicken.

Byron Nelson

On his expansive girth – When I tee the ball where I can see it, I can't hit it. And when I put it where I can hit it, I can't see it.

Jackie Gleason

Thinking you can win the Bing Crosby Pro-Am with a high handicap makes as much sense as leaving the porch light on for Jimmy Hoffa.

Phil Harris

I only see Charley Pride when we get to the greens. Charley hits some good woods – most of them trees.

Glen Campbell

Club Soda

For most amateurs the best wood in the bag is the pencil.

Chi Chi Rodriguez

You can't hit a good five iron when you're thinking about a six iron on the back swing.

Charles Coody

The only thing you should force in a golf swing is the club back into the bag.

Byron Nelson

A professional will tell you the amount of flex you need in the shaft of your club. The more the flex, the more strength you will need to break the thing over your knee.

Stephen Baker

Course Language

On designing golf courses – Every hole should be a difficult par and a comfortable bogey.

Robert T. Jones

On St Andrews Royal and Ancient Golf Club – I'm interested in the modern, not the Ancient ... There's nothing wrong with the St Andrews course that 100 bulldozers couldn't put right. The Old Course needs a dry clean and a press.
Ed Furgol

Until you play it, St Andrews looks like the sort of real estate you couldn't give away.
Sam Snead

My most common mistake at St Andrews is just turning up.
Mark James

After a calm day at St Andrews – We've had it easy. When it blows here, even the seagulls walk.
Nick Faldo

St Andrews 13th (Hole o' Cross Coming Home) – It's a great golf hole. It gives you a million options, not one of them worth a damn.
Tom Kite (1990)

St Andrews 17th (The Road Hole) – The reason the Road Hole is the greatest par four in the world is because it's a par five.
Ben Crenshaw *Sports Illustrated* (1984)

Also on the Road Hole – The most famous and infamous hole. As a planner and builder of golf holes worldwide, I have no hesitation in allowing that if one built such a hole today you would be sued for incompetence.
Peter Thompson *Golf Digest* (1984)

I don't know who designed it [the Road Hole], but I hear he's escaped.
Mark James

Carnoustie is like an ugly, old hag who speaks the truth no matter how painful. But it's only when you add up your score you hear exactly what she thinks of you.
Tom Watson

Muirfield without a wind is like a lady undressed. No challenge.
Tom Watson (1987)

Someone once said that nobody murders Troon. The way I played the Open they couldn't even arrest me for second degree manslaughter.
Lee Trevino (1973)

The par here at Sunningdale is 70 and anything under that will mean a score in the 60s.
Steve Rider

Augusta is the closest thing to heaven for a golfer – and it's just about as hard to get into.
Joe Geshwiler *San Francisco Examiner* (1983)

If there's a golf course in heaven, I hope it's like Augusta National. I just don't want an early tee time.
Gary Player

Amen Corner [at Augusta] looks like something that fell from heaven, but it plays like something straight out of hell.
Gary van Sickle

On the sloping greens at Sawgrass – I saw Sir Edmund Hillary out there, and he had to walk around the greens.

Tom Weiskopf *USA Today* **(1983)**

Sawgrass 17th (the par three island hole) – The easiest par five on the course.

John Mahaffey (1984)

Sawgrass 17th again – Every course needs a hole that puckers your rear end.

Johnny Miller (1984)

And again – The only way to improve it would be to put the green on a barge and have it float around the lagoon.

Dale Hayes (1984)

Sawgrass 18th – If you birdie the 18th, do you get a free game?

John Mahaffey

Oakmont Country Club – Most people seem to have fun here ... even when they're lining up their fourth putt.

Banks Smith

Winged Foot Golf Club, New York – The greens are harder than a whore's heart.

Sam Snead

Pebble Beach is so exclusive even the Samaritans have an unlisted number.

Peter Dobereiner (1981)

Pebble Beach is a 300-acre unplayable lie.

Jim Murray

Pebble Beach 14th – The only thing gonna stick around that hole is a dart! Yesterday I was on in three, off in four. They oughta put one of them miniature windmills on this thing and charge 50 cents to play it.

Lee Trevino (1978)

Pebble Beach and Cypress Point make you want to play golf, they're such interesting and enjoyable layouts. Spyglass Hill, now that's different; that makes you want to go fishing.

Jack Nicklaus

Southern Hills, Tulsa 5th – This hole is 614 yards. You don't need a road map for this one, you need a passport.

Jay Cronley

Alaska would be an ideal place for a golf course – mighty few trees and damn few ladies' foursomes.

Rex Lardner *Out of the Bunker* **(1960)**

On the state of the course used for the German Open – For £500,000, you'd play on a runway.

Colin Montgomerie (1990)

They all lived in houses backing onto golf courses and all boasted, 'there are fairways at the bottom of the garden'.

Frank Muir *Oh My Word*

Death Traps

I adore the game of golf. I won't ever retire. I'll play until I die. Then I want them to roll me into a bunker, cover me with sand and make sure nobody's ball lands in there for a while.
Lee Trevino (1985)

Exercise? I get it on a golf course. When I see my friends collapse, I run for the paramedics.
Red Skelton

After lightning had postponed play in the 1983 US Masters – We don't want to get anybody killed. Of course, if we could pick which ones, it might be a different story.
Hord Hardin (1983)

Define Intervention

The definition of the average golfer is: one who starts at six, shouts 'Fore!', takes five, and puts down a three.
Anon

A compulsive golfer is a crackputt.
Anon

Golf: an awkward set of bodily contortions designed to produce a graceful result.
Tommy Armour

Fairway: that which a player playing six on a long hole is heard to answer when asked how far it is to the flag.
Tim Brooke-Taylor *Golf Bag* **(1988)**

Stance: the position in which one stands immediately before clubbing an innocent tee to death.
Tim Brooke-Taylor *Ibid*

Mulligan: invented by an Irishman who wanted to hit one more 20-yard grounder.
Jim Bishop (1970)

Gimme: an agreement between two losers who can't putt.
Jim Bishop

Golfing vacations are tee leaves.
Raymond J. Cvikota

A golfing trophy is merely proof of the putting.
Shelby Friedman

A dedicated golfer can be said to be a divotee.
Charles McGee Jr.

A golf course manager is the keeper of lawn order.
Erica H. Stux

A Lorena Bobbitt: a nasty slice.
Gary McCord (1994)

Dog Legs

A golfer is a guy who can walk eight miles with a heavy bag of clubs, but when he gets home he expects his dog to fetch his slippers.
Anon

There are two things not long for this world – dogs that chase cars and pro golfers who chip for pars.

Lee Trevino

Dress Code

No golfer ever swung too slow. No golfer ever played too fast. No golfer ever dressed too plainly.

Henry Beard *Mulligan's Law* **(1994)**

Those golfers who look as though they got dressed in the dark should be penalised two strokes each for offending the public eye.

Doug Sanders

Doug Sanders' outfit has been described as looking like the aftermath of a direct hit on a pizza factory.

Dave Marr (1983)

A dozen years later, on David Duval's multi-coloured shirt – It looks like a direct hit on a pizza factory. **Dave Marr, BBC TV (1995)**

To which, Marr's co-commentator Peter Alliss replied: Mind you. If you saw Claudia Schiffer wearing it, you'd think it looked all right.

When Bill Clinton played golf ... he wore jogging shoes, and his shirt was hanging out over painter's pants. Golf needs Clinton like it needs a case of ringworm.

Rick Reilly *Sports Illustrated* **(1992)**

If this was any other tournament than the Masters, I'd have shot 66. But I was choking out there. The Green Jacket plays castanets with your knees.

Chi Chi Rodriguez

I'd give up golf if I didn't have so many sweaters.

Bob Hope

When I retire, I'm going to get a pair of grey slacks, a white shirt, a striped tie, a blue blazer, a case of dandruff and go stand on the first tee so I can be a USGA official.

Lee Trevino

Before the Ryder Cup – The only thing that scares me is the Americans' dress sense.

Mark James (1993)

Golf is not a sport. Golf is men in ugly pants, walking.

Rosie O'Donnell

Mere dregs of the golfing world who enter competitions for the hell of the thing or because they know they look well in sports clothes.

P. G. Wodehouse *Feet of Clay* **(1950)**

Golf is a game where white men can dress up as pimps and get away with it.

Robin Williams (1986)

'Play It As It Lies' is one of the fundamental dictates of golf. The other one is 'Wear It If It Clashes'.

Henry Beard *Golfing* **(1985)**

Drugs

Our guess is that the inventor of scopolamine, the truth-forcing drug, grew weary of listening to golf scores.

Colorado Springs Gazette

Drugs are very much a part of professional sport, but when you think about it, golf is the only sport where the players aren't penalised for being on grass.

Bob Hope

The PGA tour has a simple test to see if a player is on drugs – if Isao Aoki speaks and the player understands him, the player is on something.

Bob Hope

When Jack Nicklaus told me I was playing Seve Ballesteros [in the Ryder Cup singles], I took so many pills that I was glad they didn't have drug tests for golfers.

Fuzzy Zoeller (1983)

Fun Day Mental

The fun you get from golf is in direct ratio to the effort you don't put into it.

Bob Allen (1950)

Only the other day I actually saw someone *laugh* on a posh golf course in Surrey.

Michael Green *Even Coarser Sport* **(1978)**

On being paired with Lanny Wadkins – Cripes! They're going to have to hire a third person just to smile for us.

Curtis Strange

Of course, Nick Faldo is as neurotic as a long-tailed cat in a room full of rocking chairs, and pretty much No Fun ... you wouldn't want him for a brother-in-law, but he won the Ryder Cup.

***Total Sport* (1995)**

Golf Curses

Golf is a game of expletives not deleted.
Irving Gladstone

The way I putted today, I must've been reading the greens in Spanish and putting them in English.
Homero Blancas (1970)

I learn English from American pros, so that is why I speak so bad. I call it PGA English.
Roberto de Vicenzo

The interesting thing about a Coarse Golfer's language is that to listen to him one would think that his bad shots came as a surprise.
Michael Green *The Art of Coarse Golf* **(1967)**

Gripping Stuff

If some players took a fork to their mouths the way they take the club back they'd starve to death.
Sam Snead

A weak left hand? That's all right, I take cheques with the other one.

Bobby Locke

Golfers don't fist fight. They cuss a bit. But they wouldn't punch anything or anybody. They might hurt their hands and have to change their grip.

Dan Jenkins *Dead Solid Perfect* (1974)

Handicaps

Handicap: a device for collective bargaining on the first tee.

Anon

It is as easy to lower your handicap as it is to reduce your hat size.

Henry Beard *Mulligan's Law* (1994)

Hazard A Guess

Jack Spratt could only drive, his wife could only putt. So between them both, you see, they had a lot of trouble in bunkers.

Anon

The difference between a sand trap and water is the difference between a car crash and an airplane crash. You have a chance of recovering from a car crash.

Robert T. Jones

Never wash your ball on the tee of a water hole.

Henry Beard *Mulligan's Law* (1994)

After hitting two balls into the water – By God, I've got a good mind to jump in and make it four.

Simon Hobday (1994)

Heaven's Gait

After much trouble in a Muirfield bunker – I wouldn't say God couldn't have got out of it, but he'd have had to throw it.

Arnold Palmer (1987)

On how to play through a lightning storm – Hold up a one iron and walk. Not even God can hit a one iron.

Lee Trevino

If I'm on the course and lightning starts, I get inside fast. If God wants to play through, let him.

Bob Hope

God listens to me everywhere – except on the golf course.

Billy Graham

Statisticians estimate that crime among good golfers is lower than in any class of the community except possibly bishops.

P. G. Wodehouse

Hole In One

Playing with your spouse on the golf course runs almost as great a marital risk as getting caught playing with someone else's anywhere else.

Peter Andrews

Golf is like an 18-year-old girl with the big boobs. You know it's wrong but you can't keep away from her.
Val Doonican

Golf and sex are about the only things you can enjoy without being good at either.
Jimmy Demaret

Love has had a lot of press-agenting from the oldest times, but there are higher, nobler things than love. A woman is only a woman, but a hefty drive is still a slosh.
P.G. Wodehouse *A Woman Is Only a Woman*

Golf and masturbation have at least one thing in common. Both are a lot more satisfying to do than they are to watch.
Anon

The Hole Is More Than The Sum Of The Putts

A golf player is someone who can drive 70 miles an hour in heavy traffic with perfect ease; but blows up on a two-foot putt if somebody coughs.
Anon

Putting is clutch city. Usually my putting touch deserts me under pressure. From five feet in to the hole you are in the throw-up zone.
Dave Hill

I'm having putting troubles. It's not the the putter, it's the puttee.
Frank Beard

I'd rather watch a cabbage grow, than a man worrying his guts over a two-foot putt.
Michael Parkinson

Show me a man with both feet firmly planted on the ground and I'll show you a man making a crucial putt on the 18th green.
Herm Albright

The greens are so fast I have to hold my putter over the ball and hit it with the shadow.
Sam Snead

I once shot a wild elephant in Africa, 30 yards away and it didn't hit the ground until it was right at my feet. I wasn't a bit scared, but a four-foot putt scares me to death.
Sam Snead (1965)

When a golfer these days misses a 40-foot putt, he grimaces and agonises like a cowboy struck in the heart by an Indian arrow.
Ben Hogan (1975)

I enjoy the 'oohs' and 'aahs' from the gallery when I hit my drives. But I'm getting pretty tired of the 'aaws' and 'uhhs' when I miss the putt.
John Daly

After missing a very long putt – I was on the dance floor, but I couldn't hear the band.
Chi Chi Rodriguez

On refusing to use a long-handled putter – If I'm going to putt and miss, I want to look good doing it.
Chi Chi Rodriguez

Why am I using a new putter? Because the old one didn't float too well.
Craig Stadler (1983)

A tap-in is a putt that is short enough to be missed one-handed.
Henry Beard *Golfing* (1985)

The fellows today play too much golf. They burn themselves out. And on their tombstones it says: 'Here lies a millionaire. The downhill putts got him.'
Gene Sarazen

The golf game isn't over till the last putt drops.
Cary Middlecoff

Just Not Cricket

A golf shot entails merely hitting a half-volley straight back to the bowler without giving a catch.
Henry Longhurst

Golf is a game to be played between cricket and death.
Colin Ingleby-McKenzie

Keeping Up Appearances

I have a furniture problem. My chest has fallen into my drawers.
Billy Casper

It takes a lot of guts to play this game, and by looking at Billy Casper, you can tell he certainly has a lot of guts.
Gary Player

Colin Montgomerie has a face like a warthog that has been stung by a wasp.
David Feherty (1992)

Corey Pavin is a little on the slight side. When he goes through a turnstile, nothing happens.
Jim Moriarty (1984)

If you took me away from the golf tour, I'd be just another pretty face, but I'd like to see Bo Derek after 18 holes in 100-degree weather. Those cornrows and beads would be history.
Jan Stephenson (1982)

On partnering Calvin Peete and Lee Trevino in the US Open – Those nice white folks looked down the 18th fairway from the clubhouse windows and thought we were some kind of civil rights march stomping towards them. Or maybe they thought we had come to steal their hubcaps.
Chi Chi Rodriguez

Ladies' Tee-Hees

'After all, golf is only a game,' said Millicent. Women say these things without thinking. It does not mean that there is a kink in their character. They simply don't realise what they are saying.
P. G. Wodehouse *Order by Golf* (1922)

A good one-iron shot is about as easy to come by as an understanding wife.

Dan Jenkins

After he had won the Million Dollar Challenge in South Africa – I asked my wife if she wanted a Versace dress, diamonds or pearls as a present and she said, 'No!'. When I asked her what she did want, she said a divorce, but I told her I wasn't intending to spend that much.

Nick Faldo (1995)

Time can run backwards if there's a woman on the course.

Henry Beard *Mulligan's Law* **(1994)**

There are two things that guys on tour do not like: playing in the wind and me dating their sisters.

Gary McCord

Lucky Charm

The fourth hole found him four down and one had the feeling that he was lucky not to be five.

P. G. Wodehouse *Excelsior* **(1950)**

Man blames fate for other accidents but feels personally responsible for a hole in one.

Martha Beckman

The hardest shot is the chip at 90 yards from the green where the ball has to be played against an oak tree, bounces back into a sandtrap, hits a stone, bounces onto the green, and then rolls into the cup. That shot is so difficult, I have only made it once.

Zeppo Marx

Money Matters

Sam Snead's got more money buried underground than I ever made on top. He's got gophers in his backyard that subscribe to 'Fortune'. He's packed more coffee cans than Brazil.

Arnold Palmer

I plan to win so much money this year, my caddie's gonna finish in the Top 20 money winners.

Lee Trevino

Pressure is when you're playing for $10 when you don't have a dime in your pocket.

Lee Trevino

Some guys get so nervous playing for their own money, the greens don't need fertilising for a year.

Dave Hill *Teed Off* **(1977)**

Unless his putting stroke deserts him, Seve Ballesteros should become the richest Spaniard since Queen Isabella.

Jim Murray *Los Angeles Times* **(1976)**

Your financial cost of playing golf can best be figured out when you realise if you were to devote the same time and energy to business instead of golf, you would be a millionaire in approximately six weeks.
Buddy Hackett

Name Dropping

According to locker-room lore, the name golf arose by default – all the other four-letter words had already been taken.
George Pepper

On the length of time it takes to sign his autograph – Sometimes I wish my name was Tom Kite.
Ian Baker-Finch (1995)

On a barren run of form – The American players have a new name for the 'Great White Shark'. Greg Norman is referred to as the 'Carp'.
Guy Hodgson *Independent on Sunday* **(1990)**

Perhaps if I dyed my hair peroxide blonde and called myself the 'Great White Tadpole' people would take more notice of me.
Ian Woosnam (1978)

Gay Brewer sounds like a fag winemaker from Modesto.
Jimmy Demaret

Since his divorce, Fred Couples is now known as Fred Singles.
Bernard Guirk (1993)

Nineteenth Hole

Scotland is a peculiar land that is the birthplace of golf and sport salmon fishing, a fact which may explain why it is also the birthplace of whisky.
Henry Beard *An Angler's Dictionary* **(1983)**

The first time I played the Masters I was so nervous I drank a bottle of rum before I teed off. I shot the happiest 83 of my life.
Chi Chi Rodriguez

Watching a golf tournament is different from attending other sports arenas. For one thing, the drunks are spread out in a larger area.
Don Wade

I have never led the tour in money winnings, but I have many times in alcohol consumption.
Fuzzy Zoeller

Oldest Swingers In Town

Some of these legends have been around golf a long time. When they mention a good grip, they're talking about their dentures.
Bob Hope

On the introduction of the Senior Skins Game – I'm waiting for the Senile Skins Game.
Bob Hope

On becoming eligible for the Senior Tour – Why would I want to be out there with all those young guns? No sense playing the flat bellies when you can play the round bellies.

Lee Trevino (1989)

One of the nice things about the Senior Tour is that we can take a cart and a cooler. If your game is not going well, you can always have a picnic.

Lee Trevino

Over Particular

After Jack Nicklaus shot an 83 in the Open – All my life I wanted to play like Jack Nicklaus and now I do.

Paul Harvey, ABC TV (1981)

A triple bogey is three strokes more than par, four strokes more than par is a quadruple bogey, five more than par is a quintuple, six is a sextuple, seven is a throwuple, eight is a blowuple, and nine is a ohshutuple.

Henry Beard *Golfing* **(1985)**

After her tee shot bounced off a tree and nestled in her bra – I'll take a two-shot penalty, but I'll be damned if I'm going to play the ball where it lies.

Elaine Johnson (1992)

I'm playing like Tarzan – but scoring like Jane.

Chi Chi Rodriguez

Oh! The dirty little pill
Went rolling over the hill
And rolled right into a bunker.
From there to the green,
I took thirteen
And then, by God, I sunk her!
Traditional verse

Ferdinand Magellan went round the world in 1512 – which isn't too many strokes when you consider the distance.
Joe Laurie Jr

Walter Hagen once said that every golfer can expect to have four bad shots in a round and when you do, just put them out of your mind. This, of course, is hard to do when you're not even off the first tee when you've had them.
Jim Murray

Percentage Golf

Golf is a lot like taxes – you drive hard to get to the green and wind up in the hole.
Anon

I played so badly I got a get-well card from the Inland Revenue Service.
Johnny Miller (1977)

Income tax has made more liars out of the American people than golf.
Will Rogers

Phonetiquette

I'm hitting the driver so good, I gotta dial the operator for long distance after I hit it.
Lee Trevino

A distinguished professor of pathology, who recently holed out in one at the fourth at Walton Heath, thus opening the round 4, 3, 7, 1, 4, 4, 4, asks whether he is the only man in history to have started a round of golf with his own telephone number.

Henry Longhurst

Pins And Needles

The uglier a man's legs are the better he plays golf.

H.G. Wells *Bealby*

The only time Nick Faldo opens his mouth is to change feet.

David Feherty (1992)

After injuring her foot – It was stupid. I learned a lesson. When you have a fight with a club, the club always wins.

Patti Hayes

Reading Matter

To improve my golf, I once read one of those great involved books on positive thinking. I gave up when I heard the author had committed suicide.

Nick Job (1982)

On his proposed book titles – The first one is called *How to Get the Most Distance out of Your Shanks* and the other is *How to Take the Correct Stance on Your Fourth Putt.*

Lee Trevino

The nice things about these golf books is that they usually cancel each other out. One book tells you to keep your eye on the ball; the next says not to bother. Personally, in the crowd I play with, a better idea is to keep your eye on your partner.

Jim Murray

Duffers who consistently shank their balls are urged to buy and study *Shanks – No Thanks* by R. K. Hoffman, or in extreme cases, M. S. Howard's excellent *Tennis for Beginners.*

Henry Beard *Golfing* **(1985)**

The entire handbook can be reduced to three rules:
One: you do not touch your ball from the time you tee it up to the moment you pick it out of the hole.
Two: don't bend over when you are in the rough.
Three: when you are in the woods, keep clapping your hands.

Charles Price *Esquire*

Title of book – *Alliss Through The Looking Glass.*

Peter Alliss

Sportsmanship

It's good sportsmanship to not pick up lost golf balls while they are still rolling.

Mark Twain

If you think it's hard meeting new people, try picking up the wrong golf ball.

Jack Lemmon (1986)

The Coarse Golfer is one who shouts 'Fore!' when he putts.

Michael Green *The Art of Coarse Golf* **(1967)**

The number of shots taken by an opponent who is out of sight is equal to the square root of the sum of the number of curses heard plus the number of swishes.

Michael Green

Golf is the infallible test … The man who can go into a patch of rough alone, with the knowledge that only God is watching him, and play his ball where it lies is the man who will serve you faithfully and well.

P. G. Wodehouse *The Clicking of Cuthbert* **(1922)**

Few pleasures on earth match the feeling that comes from making a loud bodily-function noise just as a guy is about to putt.

Dave Barry

Straight Down The Middle

In baseball you hit your home run over the right-field fence, the left-field fence, the centre-field fence. Nobody cares. In golf everything has got to be right over second base.

Ken Harrelson

Yes, Nick Faldo's boring. He's never in the trees or in the water.

Fred Couples (1993)

I wouldn't bet anyone against Byron Nelson. The only time he left the fairway was to pee in the bushes.

Jackie Burke

Seve Ballesteros drives into territory Daniel Boone couldn't find.

Fuzzy Zoeller

I'd like to see the fairways more narrow. Then everybody would have to play from the rough, not just me.

Seve Ballesteros (1979)

After Europe won the 1995 Ryder Cup – I only played three matches and hit only three fairways. My biggest contribution was to get the team colours for Sunday changed from green to my lucky blue.

Seve Ballesteros (1995)

Like all Saturday foursomes it is in difficulties. One of the patients is zigzagging about the fairway like a liner pursued by submarines.

P. G. Wodehouse *On Golf* **(1973)**

My golf game's gone off so much that when I went fishing a couple of weeks ago my first cast missed the lake.

Ben Crenshaw (1977)

Swing Low

Anyone who would pass up an opportunity to see Sam Snead swing a golf club at a golf ball would pull down the shades when driving past the Taj Mahal.

Jim Murray *Los Angeles Times*

Corey Pavin is the only golfer whose practice swing is worse than his actual swing.
Johnny Miller (1995)

I was swinging like a toilet door on a prawn trawler.
David Feherty (1993)

Lee Trevino is the only man I know who talks on his backswing.
Charley McClendon *Sports Illustrated* **(1972)**

My golf swing is like ironing a shirt. You get one side smoothed out, turn it over and there is a big wrinkle on the other side. You iron that side, turn it over and there's another wrinkle.
Tom Watson (1987)

Hubert Green swings like a drunk trying to find a keyhole in the dark.
Jim Murray *Los Angeles Times*

Gay Brewer swings the club in a figure of eight. If you didn't know better, you'd swear he was trying to kill snakes.
Dave Hill

My favourite shots are the practice swing and the conceded putt. The rest cannot be mastered.
Lord Robertson

Technique

Watching Sam Snead practise hitting golf balls is like watching a fish practise swimming.
John Schlee *Golf Digest* **(1977)**

Seve Ballesteros goes after a golf course the way a lion goes after a zebra.
Jim Murray *Los Angeles Times*

I keep thinking that I might go out and play like Jack Nicklaus, but instead, it's more like Jacques Tati.
David Feherty (1992)

It took me 17 years to get 3,000 hits in the baseball park. I did it in one afternoon on the golf course.
Henry 'Hank' Aaron

You can talk to a fade but a hook won't listen.
Lee Trevino

They say I'm famous for my chip shots. Sure, when I hit 'em right, they land just so, like a butterfly with sore feet.
Lee Trevino

No matter how hard I try, I just can't seem to break 64.
Jack Nicklaus

The difference between a good golf shot and a bad one is the same as the difference between a beautiful woman and a plain one – a matter of millimetres.
Ian Fleming *Goldfinger* **(1959)**

In Britain, you skip the ball, hop it, hump it, run it, hit under it, on top of it and then hope for the right bounce.
Doug Sanders *Sports Illustrated* **(1984)**

I never did see the sense in keeping my head down. The only reason I play golf is to see where the ball goes.
Charles Price *Golfer-at-Large* **(1982)**

I have one fault when I play golf, I really admit it.
I find I'm too close to the ball – I mean after I hit it!
Maurice Seitter

The average golfer doesn't play golf. He attacks it.
Jackie Burke

The golfer who stands at the ball as rigid as a statue usually becomes a monumental failure.
Dick Aultman

The most exquisitely satisfying act in the world of golf is that of throwing a club. The full backswing, the delayed wrist action, the flowing follow-through, followed by that unique whirring sound, reminiscent only of a passing flock of starlings, are without parallel in sport.
Henry Longhurst

Some players would complain if they had to play on Dolly Parton's bedspread.
Jimmy Demaret

Tee Time

If there's a faster way to turn a Jekyll into a Hyde than by handing a man the driver, we don't know of it.
Lew Fishman

My backswing off the first tee had put him in mind of an elderly lady of dubious morals trying to struggle out of a dress too tight around the shoulders.
Patrick Campbell

If Jack Nicklaus had to play my tee shots, he couldn't break 80. He'd be a pharmacist with a string of drugstores in Ohio.
Lee Trevino

When John Daly hits an iron he takes a cubic yard of Kent as well. His divots go further than my drives.
David Feherty (1993)

John Daly's driving is unbelievable. I don't go that far on my holidays.
Ian Baker-Finch (1992)

On John Daly's driving power – Man! I can't even point that far!
Gay Brewer

Television

If you want to take long walks, take long walks. If you want to hit things with sticks, hit things with sticks. But there's no excuse for combining the two and putting the results on television. Golf is not so much a sport as an insult to lawns.
National Lampoon (1979)

I don't like to watch golf on television because I can't stand people who whisper.
David Brenner (1977)

I would rather play Hamlet on Broadway with no rehearsal rather than play TV golf.
Jack Lemmon

Win, Lose Or Tie

After helping Argentina defeat England in the World Cup – Like Maradona, I too used my hand, but only to pick my birdies out of the hole.
Vincente Fernandez (1986)

On being asked, before his final round, what he had to shoot to win the tournament – The rest of the field.
Roger Maltbie

After a tie saw Europe retain the Ryder Cup – Big Mouth Yanks Get Their Own Butts Kicked.
***Daily Star* headline (1989)**

Show me a man who is a good loser and I'll show you a man who is playing golf with his boss.
Nebraska Smoke-Eater

Show me a good loser and I'll show you a seldom winner.
Sam Snead

In 1981, Tom Sieckmann won the Philippine Open, the Thailand Open and the Singapore Open, leaving him second only to the US Marines for victories in the Pacific.
Gary Nuhm *Dayton Daily News*

On losing to Greg Norman on the second extra hole in the World Matchplay – I played crap, he played crap. He just out-crapped me.
Wayne Grady (1990)

After Costantino Rocca's singles defeat had 'lost' the Ryder Cup for Europe – Italy cost us two world wars. Now they have cost us the Ryder Cup.
Anon German spectator (1993)

Golf Rhymes

They say that President Taft,
When hit by a golf ball, once laughed
And said, 'I'm not sore,
Although he called Fore
The place where he hit me was aft!'
Anon

And the wind shall say 'Here were decent godless people;
Their only monument the asphalt road
And a thousand lost golf balls.'
T.S. Eliot

Golfing takes energy, also cash –
Just two of the things you must bring it;
A golf club's a great institution
If you are able to swing it!
George O. Ludcke

While tearing off
A game of golf
I may make a play for the caddy.
But when I do
I don't follow through
'Cause my heart belongs to Daddy.
Cole Porter (1938)

"Horse Racing"

AFTER HIS FALL, CARL LLEWELLYN IS OK. HE'S JUST WALKED INTO THE AMBULANCE.
Peter O'Sullevan, BBC TV (1994)

Better Beware

No one has ever bet enough on a winning horse.
Richard Sasuly

A racetrack is a place where windows clean people.
Danny Thomas

In most betting shops you will see three windows marked 'Bet Here', but only one window with the legend 'Pay Out'.
Jeffrey Bernard

Any money I put on a horse is a sort of insurance policy to prevent it from winning.
Frank Richardson

Remember, Lady Godiva put all she had on a horse and she lost her shirt!
W. C. Fields

If in the paddock the owner is surrounded by a herd of young children, don't back his horse. But if the owner is accompanied by a beautiful lady, plunge to the hilt.
Robert Morley

I wouldn't bet on a horse unless he came up to my house and told me to himself.
Eubie Blake (1975)

In betting on races, there are two elements that are never lacking – hope as hope, and an incomplete recollection of the past.
Edward V. Lucas (1951)

The reason Con loses at the races, while he always wins at cards, is that he can't shuffle the horses!
The Jockey Who Laughs

Losers walking around with money in their pockets are always dangerous, not to be trusted. Some horse always reaches out and grabs them.
Bill Barich

The only exercise I get is walking to the betting office.
Peter O'Sullevan *Daily Telegraph* **(1994)**

Horse sense is what keeps horses from betting on what people will do.
Raymond Nash

It's one thing to ask your bank manager for an overdraft to buy 500 begonias for the borders in Haslemere, but quite another to seek financial succour to avail oneself of the 5-2 they're offering on Ile de Bourbon for the St Leger.
Jeffrey Bernard (1978)

Fortunately my wife is understanding. When I come home from the races she never asks any questions, if I tell her I just ate a $380 hot dog.
Tim Conway

They head the list of bad to bet on:
But I insist they're worse to get on
Richard Armour

Biblical

To amateur jockey Jim Old – If Jesus Christ rode his flaming donkey like you just rode that horse, then he deserved to be crucified.
Fred Rimell

Secretariat and Riva Ridge are the most famous pair of stablemates since Joseph and Mary.
Dick Schaap

Breeding Nuisance

You need luck as well as good blood lines to produce a horse like Secretariat. It's a funny thing. For instance, Secretariat has a half-sister who looks like a potential winner. But he also has a half-sister who couldn't outrun a fat man going downhill.
Helen Tweedy

Artificial insemination is a crazy idea. Who wants 100 Mill Reefs anyway?
Richard Baerlein *The Observer* **(1978)**

After one of them has won the Kentucky Derby, any breeding expert can sit down and show you just why he won – from his pedigree. The only trouble is, the expert can't do it before the race.
Phil Chinn

Brigadier Gerard did not win the Derby because he did not run in it. He did not run in it because he was not bred for it. He wasn't bred for it because I couldn't afford it.
John Hislop (1972)

Thoroughbreds are superior horses which sneer at other horses who are not in their *Who's Who* – the *General Stud Book*. Their telephone numbers are ex-directory. They often gather for many social events such as Ascot when they study one another's clothes and general turn-out.

Rintoul Booth (1975)

What a pity people don't take as much trouble with their own breeding as intelligent racehorse owners do. But then I suppose it is bordering on fascism to think like that.

Jeffrey Bernard *The Spectator* (1994)

The lower classes are such fools,
They waste their money on the pools.
I bet, of course, but that's misleading.
One must encourage bloodstock
breeding.

Bernard Fergusson

Criminal Behaviour

Instead of a month's jail someone should be sentenced to reading *The Sporting Life* on non-racing days.

Lord Wigg (1959)

Derby Shyer

It is good to breed Derby winners because they will in time beget other horses capable of the same splendid and useless triumphs.

***Bentley's Quarterly Review* (1859)**

There is only one race greater than the Jews – and that is the Derby.

Victor Sassoon

I never rode a Derby that wasn't a bit like a polo match – only with more horses.

Jack Leach

After winning the Derby on Tulyar –
What did I Tulyar!

Charlie Smirke (1952)

After winning the Derby aged just 18 –
Why all the fuss? After all, the Derby is just another race.

Lester Piggott (1954)

Fillies and Mares

I see no particular objection to giving women a chance to ride in races now and again ... such races should be on the Flat and be placed last on the card so that those racegoers not interested can return home for tea and *Magic Roundabout*.

Roger Mortimer

Women jockeys are a pain. Jumping's a man's game. They are not built like us. Most of them are as strong as half a disprin.

Steve Smith-Eccles (1988)

A horse doesn't know whether the rider on his back wears a dress or pants away from the track.

Diane Crump

On the unsuitability of female jockeys –
Their bottoms are the wrong shape.

Lester Piggott *The Guinness Book of*
Great Jockeys **(1992)**

Food and Drink

I understand it is 13–8 against Egon
Ronay publishing a *Good Betting Shop*
Food Guide by 1997.

Clement Freud *Sporting Life* **(1994)**

On trainer Peter Chisman – He didn't
drink me under the table, he drank me
under the Grandstand.

Jeffrey Bernard (1979)

I have stood in a bar in Lambourn and
been offered, in the space of five
minutes, a poached salmon, a leg of a
horse, a free trip to Chantilly, marriage, a
large unsolicited loan, ten tips for a ten-
horse race, two second-hand cars, a
fight, and the copyright to a dying
jockey's life story.

Jeffrey Bernard (1979)

Win or lose
We'll have a booze

Attrib to Ken Oliver

Governing Bodies

The Jockey Club have issued a writ
against the Texan who introduced
Cabbage Patch dolls. They claim they
have been making them for years – and
calling them stewards.

John Francome (1983)

Someone suggested that the Jockey
Club Race Planning Committee
consisted of a table and four chairs – and
I bet they've got woodworm.

Jenny Pitman (1989)

With some justification the Jockey Club
has been described as 'the purest
example of the 18th century to survive in
Britain'.

John Purvis

Giving a computer to the Tote would be
like giving an atom bomb to a baby.

Lord Wigg *The Sun* **(1969)**

If Lord Wigg mistook us for a dinosaur,
we no longer take him for a taxidermist.

The National Association of Bookmakers

Stewards are, on the whole, simple folk.
Most them come from a social class in
which inbreeding has taken its toll.

Paul Haigh *Racing Post* **(1994)**

Eventually the pool from which stewards
were selected was extended beyond the
registered blind, the chronically inbred
and those whose ear trumpets or
searing gout problems rendered them
half-sharp or pathologically vicious.

Alistair Down *Weekender* **(1994)**

After the King George VI Chase – It appears that within half a mile of the Jockey Club's HQ at Portman Square any man wishing to be hit with a whip with the same intensity as Adrian Maguire hit Barton Bank would have to pay £40 for the privilege.

C. Williams, letter to *Racing Post* (1993)

Grand National

The 1980 Grand National – a tremendous race, with four finishers out of 30 starters, so that by the end there were far more BBC commentators than horses.

Clive James *The Observer* (1980)

Having seen the Grand National, it was always my ambition to throw a saddle over Mrs Mirabelle Topham [the racecourse owner] and ride her over those appalling Aintree fences.

Arthur Askey *Before Your Very Eyes* (1975)

Ten of the most pointless things in the world:
No. 3: Urging your horse on while watching the Grand National on TV.

Journolists *Mail on Sunday*

On animal rights protesters – If they get on the course, let the horses gallop over them. That'll stop them.

Ginger McCain (1994)

The Aintree starter Simon Morant couldn't start a race for white mice.

David Nicholson

Handicap Heard All

A handicapper being a character who can dope out from the form what horses ought to win the races, and as long as his figures turn out all right, a handicapper is spoken of most respectfully by one and all, although of course when he begins missing out for any length of time as handicappers are bound to do, he is no longer spoken of respectfully, or even as a handicapper. He is spoken of as a bum.

Damon Runyon *All Horse Players Die Broke*

If you want to understand the effect of weight on a horse, try running for a bus with nothing in your hands. Then try doing it with your hands full of shopping. Then think about doing that for four and a half miles.

Jenny Pitman (1985)

On learning that Desert Orchid was more well known than the Chancellor of the Exchequer – Desert Orchid and I have a lot in common. We are both greys; vast sums of money are riding on our performance; the Opposition hopes we will fall at the first fence, and we are both carrying too much weight.

Norman Lamont (1991)

Hoarse Talk

Desert Orchid can't say he's as 'sick as a parrot', or that he won't be quoted until you've talked to his agent. As a gelding he's unlikely to make the nookie sections of the tabloids. He just sets off towards the fences and invites you to throw your spirit with him.

Brough Scott (1989)

On why horse racing is easier to cover for a sports journalist – You never have to run after the winner, asking him for a few words.

Earl Wilson

How amusing racing would be if it were not for the horses. They take people's minds off conversation.

Viscount Castlerosse *Sunday Express*

Horses Fork Horses

A real racehorse should have a head like a lady and the behind like a cook.

Jack Leach

If you could call the thing a horse. If it hadn't shown a flash of speed in the straight, it would have got mixed up with the next race.

P. G. Wodehouse *Very Good, Jeeves* **(1930)**

A loose horse is any horse sensible enough to get rid of its rider at an early stage and carry on unencumbered.

Clive James (1980)

Never catch a loose horse. You could end up holding the f**king thing all day.

Lester Piggott

On a horse that consistently hung left – The best thing you can do is put a bit of lead in his right ear, to act as a counter-balance ... with a shotgun.

Lester Piggott

It was the plainest Oaks field I have ever seen, and the paddock critic who expressed a decided preference for the horse of the policewoman on duty was no bad judge.

Roger Mortimer *The Sunday Times* **(1972)**

If a horse is no good, trade him for a dog, then shoot the dog.

Ben Jones

John McCririck: And finally, Brough, there are two or three horses in later races being heavily whispered around the ring – what I call 'psst' horses.
Brough Scott: Well, if we're going to have 'psst' horses the whole thing is going to fall apart.

Channel 4 TV

Horses are red,
Horses are blue,
Horses that lose
Are turned into glue.

Anon

After winning Ascot's Queen Alexandra Stakes on Brown Jack – If you'd been on your honeymoon, you couldn't have had a happier time.

Steve Donoghue

Red Rum is in a stable condition.
Anon newsreader *BBC Radio 5* **(1992)**

Red Rum is the greatest thing on four
legs since Pegasus.
Jean Rook

I rode Sea Pigeon in all his work – that's
why my arms are so long.
Mark Birch (1983)

I could cut through the infield and
Ruffian would still beat me.
Braulio Baeza

If I were young, fast, healthy, and had a
lot of money and my whole sex life
ahead of me, I'd retire – like Secretariat.
Dick Butkus (1973)

Secretariat is everything I am not. He is
young, he has lots of hair, he is fast, he
has a large bank account and his entire
sex life is before him.
Cy Burick *Dayton Daily News* **(1973)**

John Henry was no prize. He was back
at the knee, ungainly in appearance and
had a disposition to rival Dennis the
Menace.
Mel Snowdon (1982)

Lochsong – she's like Linford Christie ...
without the lunchbox.
Frankie Dettori (1994)

On Slip Anchor's emphatic Derby win – It
was a nice change for some of us to be
identified with a horse that applies the
Garbo principle at the right end of the
field.
Hugh McIlvanney (1985)

Jockey Shorts

Jockey (Flat): An anorexic dwarf in bright
colours who drives a large car with
cushions on the seat and blocks on the
pedals.
Jockey (Jump): Punch-drunk, nobbly,
occasionally hot-headed individual who
must be as stupid as he looks to take
100 times as many risks as the flat
counterpart for one hundredth of the
rewards.
Julian Seaman *Turfed Out* **(1988)**

There are, they say, fools, bloody fools
and men who remount in a
steeplechase.
John Oaksey

A jump jockey has to throw his heart
over the fence – and then go over and
catch it.
Dick Francis

It amazes me how well the majority of
jump jockeys ride in a race until they've
landed over the last, then how badly
most of them ride a finish. Apart from a
half-dozen, they look like coster boys
sitting on top of donkeys' behinds,
bashing about with shillelaghs.
Jack Leach *A Rider in the Stand*

I was young and fearless in those days, but always enjoyed riding at Cartmel. They used to call me 'Cartmellor', probably because I kept coming back on a stretcher.

Stan Mellor (1982)

Willie Carson, riding his 180th winner of the season, spent the last two furlongs looking over one shoulder then another, even between his legs, but there was nothing there to worry him.

Sporting Life

Possibly in answer to the above – I'm lucky because I have an athlete between my legs.

Willie Carson (1992)

I have no intention of watching undersized Englishmen perched on horses with matchstick legs race along courses planned to amuse Nell Gwynn.

Gilbert Harding

Horses and jockeys mature earlier than people – which is why horses are admitted to racetracks at the age of two, and jockeys before they are old enough to shave.

Dick Beddoes

On receiving his knighthood – Mother always told me my day was coming, but I never realised I'd end up being the shortest knight of the year.

Sir Gordon Richards

Bill Shoemaker didn't ride a horse, he joined them. Most riders beat horses as if they were guards in slave-labour camps. Shoe treated them as if he were asking them to dance.

Jim Murray *Los Angeles Times*

My horse was in the lead, coming down the home stretch, but the caddie fell off.

Samuel Goldwyn

Recapping his career – 470 winners and 5000 losers

Richard Pitman

On his varied workload – I'm riding out for every stable bar Bethlehem at the moment

Dean McKeown

Lester Squire

People ask me why I ride with my bottom in the air. Well, I've got to put it somewhere.

Lester Piggott

A good jockey doesn't need orders and a bad jockey couldn't carry them out anyway; so it's best not to give them any.

Lester Piggott

In a perfect world, I would have Lester ride for me in all the big races, but in none of the Trials.

Vincent O'Brien

Lester relishes every crisp fiver like some rare jewel, for money is his staff of life and he ekes it out as sparingly as a man faced with 50 years of unpensionable retirement.
Bill Rickaby

Jeremy Tree (trainer): I've got to speak to my old school, Lester, and tell them all I know about racing. What should I tell them?
Lester Piggott: Tell 'em you've got the flu.

Loss Adjusters

A bookie is just a pickpocket who lets you use your own hands.
Henry Morgan

I am not one of the people who believe that the main reason why a chap becomes a bookmaker is because he is too scared to steal and too heavy to become a jockey.
Noel Whitcombe

Name Dropping

If some horses merit Timeform's dreaded double squiggle for terrible performances what about the men responsible for The Mr Chris Real Dairy Cream Cake Handicap Hurdle?
Monty Court *The Weekender* (1986)

Calling home a close finish – And the judge has called for a photo, appropriately for the Bonusprint Sirenia Stakes.
Graham Goode, Channel 4 TV (1995)

Own Up

Owning a racehorse is probably the most expensive way of getting on to a racecourse for nothing.
Clement Freud *The Times* (1989)

We have been involved in racing for so long, it is astonishing we were not born with hooves.
Daniel Wildenstein (1977)

I try to keep myself in the best of company and my horses in the worst of company.
Lenny Goodman (1979)

There is little to compare with the thrill of standing next to the creature in the winner's enclosure avoiding his hooves and receiving the congratulations of the press, your trainer and friends who backed it. What makes the experience so satisfying is that you, the owner, have had absolutely nothing to do with the horse winning.
Robert Morley

You never see a pretty, unattached girl on a racecourse. But you often see positive gangs of rather unpretty ones. They are the owners or the owners' wives and they wear mink in all weathers and far too much make-up. For some odd reason, I can never work out why they always seem to be married to haulage contractors in the North, builders in the South and farmers in the West.
Jeffrey Bernard

On being asked by Channel 4's Derek Thompson if he owned horses – No, son. I don't like anything that eats while I sleep.

Larry Hagman (1986)

Comparing his San Diego Chargers football team to his horses – The horses don't have no agents, they don't call me in the morning to renegotiate after winning a race, they don't petition me for more oats, and they don't object to urine analysis.

Gene Klein

Racecourses

There are three racecourses beginning with the letter F – namely Fontwell, Folkestone and effing Plumpton.

Attributed to Fred Winter

At one time a little humdrum adultery could prove a barrier to the Royal Enclosure at Ascot, but now something rather more spectacular is required, such as hijacking a Securicor van or taking too prominent a role in a sex instruction film designed for circulation in the best preparatory schools.

Roger Mortimer *The Sunday Times* (1971)

I loathe Royal Ascot with a passion. All those people who wouldn't know which end bites trying to get spotted by Judith Chalmers, while you're trying to get the saddle down to the horse.

Charles O'Brien *The Independent* (1994)

Apart from the gloriously groomed Royal Drive down the course, Ascot, in the last five years, had slumped from a *My Fair Lady* spectacle into a vulgar and tatty farce.

Jean Rook *Daily Express* (1983)

Applying for membership of the Members' Stand at Ascot is now on a par with applying for a passport. One must have the application approved by one of the following list: Ascot annual member, member of the Jockey Club, JP, Minister of Religion, Medical Practitioner, Bank Manager, Chief Constable, Assistant Chief Constable, Barrister or Solicitor. It is a wide choice provided one is not an atheist, bankrupt, sick or in trouble with the law.

Richard Baerlein (1971)

When I die I want it to be on Ascot Gold Cup Day.

Betty Kenward *Harpers and Queen* (1979)

Ascot is so exclusive that it is the only racecourse in the world where the horses own the people.

Art Buchwald *Ordeal at Ascot*

Jumping at Ascot is like Blackpool with the tide out.

John Hislop

On Newbury's new Berkshire Grandstand – This is really one of those buildings where the best view is from in it, senses preferably anaesthetised by a stiff drink. A clumpy, Frankenstein agglomeration of pitched roofs, folksy dormers and faux Victorian conservatories that appear to have suffered a near fatal attack of Supermarket Vernacular. An overblown confection resembling a mutant cricket pavilion.

Catherine Slessor *Architectural Review* (1994)

Some people are born in circumstances which resemble being saddled in the enclosure at Epsom ... when the race is at Ripon.

Tom Crabtree

Take one measure of Goodwood, two of Salisbury, add a dash of Château setting and you have a cocktail called Chantilly, and on a cold damp day last Sunday, I left the racecourse shaken but not stirred.

Prince Pippi (1978)

The Cheltenham National Hunt Festival is an adult Christmas.

Stuart Barnes (1994)

Cheltenham's new million-plus stand is surely an improvement but if you have binoculars capable of seeing through concrete, you're advised to bring them.

Peter O'Sullevan (1979)

The simple truth is that some of our racecourses are so poorly run and unimaginatively managed, and couldn't attract extra customers if Arkle, Desert Orchid, Nijinsky and the Archangel Gabriel all appeared on the same card.

***Sporting Life* (1994)**

Trainer Spotters

Trainers by nature are seldom savers. Eat, drink and be merry – tomorrow we're bankrupt.

Ivor Herbert (1980)

The Stewards demand explanations
But listen with cynical looks.
It's obvious in their estimations
That trainers are all licensed crooks.
Anon

The only tip I can give on jumpers is – where to buy them in London.

Henry Cecil *Racing Post* (1993)

Jockular Jests

The horse I bet on
Came in so late, that it had to tiptoe into the barn not to wake the other horses.
Anon

The horse I bet on
Had four legs and flies – unfortunately it was a dead horse
Anon

A jockey was nicknamed Sunshine, because he always came after the reins.
Anon

Two racehorses were training together. One looked at the other and said, 'I can't remember your name but the pace looks familiar!'
Anon

Other Equestrian Events

There is nothing like horse-back riding to make a person feel better off.

Riding is the art of keeping a horse between yourself and the ground.
Anon

There are no handles to horses.
Stephen Leacock

Rodeoing is the only sport you can't fix. You'd have to talk to the bulls and the horses, and they wouldn't understand you.
Bill Linderman (1954)

The rodeo isn't over till the bull riders ride.
Ralph Carpenter (1978)

If I'm reincarnated, I want to come back as a bucking horse. You work 8 seconds, then eat and sleep the rest of the time.
Pete Gay

Playing polo is like trying to play golf during an earthquake.
Sylvester Stallone

Oh wasn't it naughty of Smudges?
Oh, Mummy, I'm sick with disgust.
She threw me in front of the judges,
And my silly old collarbone's bust.
John Betjeman *Hunter Trials* **(1954)**

It's awf'lly bad luck on Diana
Her ponies have swallowed their bits;
She fished down their throats with a spanner
And frightened them all into fits.
John Betjeman *Hunter Trials* **(1954)**

You might have imagined that Harvey Smith was mounted on a piece of stereo equipment, but Sanyo Music Centre, though it has a leg in each corner like certain types of radiogram, is in fact a living creature with no provision for the electronic reproduction of sound.
Clive James (1981)

At the Olympics, I love watching anything that's special as long as it doesn't have a horse in it.
Daley Thompson (1988)

Accidents Will Happen

Once an accident has started happening, you've just got enough time to say 'Sh*t, I'm having a shunt!'
James Hunt (aka Hunt the Shunt)

You win some, you lose some, you wreck some.
Dale Earnhardt

On falling off a race bike at high speed – It's kind of like tumbling around inside a giant clothes-drier.
Dave Aldane (1975)

At 180 mph, when your front wheel wants to play pogo stick, you don't do nothing. You don't sneeze, you don't hiccup, you don't even breathe. All you do is point it and hang on.
Kenny Roberts

It's hard to describe what it's like to see a stock car flying through the air knowing it's going to land on top of you.
Benny Parsons (1976)

Car Pet

Never think of your car as a cold machine, but as a hot-blooded horse.
Juan Manuel Fangio (1958)

Every car has a lot of speed in it. The trick is getting the speed out of it.

A. J. Foyt

On the Lotus race car – You get more than one of them things and you call them Loti.

Parnelli Jones

There's enough Ferraris here to eat a plate of spaghetti.

Jackie Stewart

On Williams-Renault's new design – The driver's position will be more horizontal than last year. It will be like lying in a bath with your feet on the taps, but not as comfortable.

David Coulthard (1995)

Cash Barriers

Motor racing's less of a sport these days than a commercial break doing 150 mph.

Peter Dunne *Independent on Sunday* **(1992)**

Not that I'd ever think of leaving 'ere I love England. But I do resent giving the income tax inspector 83 per cent. I tell him he's welcome to it if he went out and got on my bike and got throwed up the road at 190 mph, be in hospital for weeks, then walk around 'alf crippled for the rest of his life ... if they did that they're welcome to my money.

Barry Sheene (1979)

I get a buzz every time I sit in a racing car, every time I start up the engine ... If I was earning £1 a race, I'd still be a racing driver – just a poor one.

Nigel Mansell (1988)

Dangerous Driving

You may drive the freeway daily at top speeds with confidence and skill. But that doesn't qualify you as a race driver. Put an ordinary driver in an Indy-type race car and he'd probably crash before he got out of the pit area.

Al Unser

On the dangers of the Monte Carlo Rally – Some of the ravines are so deep that if you topple over, your clothes will be out of date by the time you hit the bottom.

Tony Pond (1986)

I had to go off the circuit twice to avoid him. I don't know what René Arnoux is doing in Formula One racing. He should be on the beach.

Thierry Boutsen (1989)

Drag On Power

If horse racing is the sport of kings, then drag racing must be the sport of queens.

Bert R. Sugar

I want to be the fastest woman in the world ... in a manner of speaking.

Shirley Muldowney (1975)

Drivers

Some drivers grow the fruit. Others just come in and pick it.

Nigel Mansell (1992)

Nigel Mansell is so brave, but such a moaner. He should have 'He Who Dares Whines' embroidered on his overalls.

Simon Barnes *The Times* **(1993)**

Nigel Mansell is someone with about as much charisma as a damp spark-plug.

Alan Hubbard *The Observer* **(1992)**

Nigel Mansell is the only man who goes to Nick Faldo for charisma lessons.

Nick Hancock *They Think It's All Over* **BBC TV (1995)**

Keke Rosberg is as calculating as a slot machine.

Louis T. Stanley

Dad taught me everything I know, but he would never tell me anything he knew.

Al Unser Jr

Nelson Piquet looks like a jockey being strapped into his car. Alan Jones looks like a commando on his way to Vietnam.

Charlie Crichton Stuart

On receiving an OBE from the British government – When I drove for British teams ... they called me 'The Tadpole' because I was too small to be a frog.

Alain Prost (1994)

On starting from the back of the grid – My dad once said that you meet a much nicer class of person there, but I'm not sure.

Damon Hill (1993)

The best classroom of all times was about two car lengths behind Juan Manuel Fangio.

Stirling Moss

I do not speak the English so good, but then I speak the driving very well.

Emerson Fittipaldi (1973)

Extreme Caution

On his race strategy – To win a race in the slowest possible time.

Jack Brabham

Never forget that you have an appointment with a man with a chequered flag at the end. You can be late if you like, but if you don't keep that appointment you might just as well not have started.

Sammy Davis (1920)

GP

Grand Prix driving is like balancing an egg on a spoon while shooting the rapids.

Graham Hill

Grand Prix motor racing is like *Punch*. It is never as good as it was.

Maxwell Boyd

On the Monaco Grand Prix – This is a very special race. It's the most colourful grand prix in the world, and it's really classy here, but if I don't win, I'm going to hate the damn joint.

Mario Andretti (1978)

Fatal Attraction

You have to treat death like any other part of life.

Tom Sneva

It is necessary to relax your muscles when you can. Relaxing your brain is fatal.

Stirling Moss

In my sport the quick are too often listed among the dead.

Jackie Stewart (1973)

My first priority is to finish above rather than beneath the ground.

James Hunt (1975)

You cannot be superstitious in this thing. Otherwise I would never start a race. If you have some lucky object, then you would not have it some day and you would have to start the race without it, and you'd get killed, right?

Giacomo Agostini (1967)

Feminine Touch

On being asked if female drivers were as strong as their male counterparts – You drive the car, you don't carry it.

Janet Guthrie

After Janet Guthrie had qualified for the Indy 500 – In company with the first lady to ever qualify at Indianapolis – gentlemen, start your engines.

Tom Hulman

I'd rather have an accident than fall in love – that's how much I love motor racing.

Lella Lombardi (1975)

On winning the Indy 500 – It sure didn't make me the million dollars people said it would, but it sure made my ex-wife happy.

Bobby Unser

Hands-On

You can always spot a motorcycle racer in a restaurant. He's the one gripping his fork with the first two fingers of his left hand.

Kenny Roberts (1973)

Measure For Measure

Racing is 99 per cent boredom and one per cent terror.

Geoff Brabham

The world land-speed record requires the minimum of skill and the maximum of courage.

Tommy Wisdom

Road Holding

Mansell handles corners better than Maradona.
Banner at Silverstone (1987)

On the lack of safety precautions at the Nürburgring – You'd have to be William Tell to hit a straw bale round here.
Barry Sheene (1974)

Sex Drive

There are only two things no man will admit he can't do well: drive a car and make love.
Stirling Moss

If a man can f**k and drive race cars, man … I mean, what else is there?
Billy Scott (1974)

I don't imagine these guys now have any problem finding girls; but I think they train more than we did. We used to use girls to train with. Now they use ropes and chinning. We trained with women.
Tim Flock (1974)

I've never seen driving as a sexual thing – I just could never consider it in that light. I think women are interested in the drivers because of the dangers, but some of us are as dull as Old Nick.
Jackie Stewart (1968)

But … four years later – Cornering is like bringing a woman to a climax. Both you and the car must work together. You start to enter the area of excitement at the corner, you set up a pace which is right for the car and after you've told it it is coming along with you, you guide it along at a rhythm which has by now become natural. Only after you've cleared the corner you can both take pleasure in knowing it's gone well.
Jackie Stewart (1972)

Spare Parts

When a V8 gets running bad, it's like it's in labour. It's only a matter of time before everything goes.
A. J. Foyt (1976)

Nobody is born with a steering wheel or a gear shift in his hand. It's something you choose to do or you don't.
Mario Andretti (1977)

WELSH RUGBY UNION CHIEFS GAVE THEIR FULL BACKING TO A JUDGE AFTER HE JAILED A VIOLENT PLAYER WHO STAMPED ON AN OPPONENT'S HEAD FOR SIX MONTHS.

Daily Post (1994)

Anglo Files

The only hope for the England rugby union team is to play it all for laughs. It would pack them in if the public address system at Twickenham was turned up full blast to record the laughs at every inept bit of passing, kicking or tackling. The nation would be in fits … and on telly the BBC would not need a commentator but just a tape of that Laughing Policeman, turning it loud at the most hilarious bits.

Jim Rivers, letter to *The Guardian* (1979)

A bomb under the West car park at Twickenham on an international day would end fascism in England for a generation.

Philip Toynbee

If the game is run properly as a professional game, you do not need 57 old farts running rugby.

Will Carling (1995)

Most Misleading Campaign of 1991: England's rugby World Cup squad, who promoted a scheme called 'Run with the Ball'. Not, unfortunately, among themselves.

Time Out (1991)

On England's new rubber training suit –
As you run around Battersea Park in
them, looking like a cross between a
member of the SAS and *Blake's Seven*,
there is always the lingering fear of
arrest.

Brian Moore (1995)

*After England had been humbled by
New Zealand in the World Cup semi-final*
– I don't know about us not having a Plan
B when things went wrong, we looked
like we didn't have a Plan A.

Geoff Cooke (1995)

England's coach Jack Rowell, an
immensely successful businessman, has
the acerbic wit of Dorothy Parker and,
according to most New Zealanders, a
similar knowledge of rugby.

Mark Reason *Total Sport* (1996)

Backs Against The Wall

Rugby backs can be identified because
they generally have clean jerseys and
identifiable partings in their hair ... come
the revolution the backs will be the first
to be lined up against the wall and shot
for living parasitically off the work of
others.

Peter Fitzsimmons *Rugby Stories* (1993)

*On his successors in the Oxford
University backs* – I've seen better
centres in a box of Black Magic.

Joe McPartlin

If I had been a winger, I might have been
daydreaming and thinking about how to
keep my kit clean for next week.

Bill Beaumont

Rugby players are either piano shifters or
piano movers. Fortunately, I am one of
those who can play a tune.

Pierre Danos

Rory Underwood: The gentleman athlete
and flightmeister.

Punch

Simon Geoghegan: The winger
resembles Mother Brown, running with
a high knee-lift and sometimes not
progressing far from the spot where he
started.

Mark Reason *Total Sport* (1996)

Peter Sterling: If Walt Disney had seen
this little man's antics, there'd have been
no Mickey Mouse.

Ray French, BBC TV (1985)

Martin Offiah: Your hands can't CATCH
what your eyes can't see.

Nike rugby boot advert (1993)

These days you have to be able to
concentrate for an hour non-stop, you're
drenched in perspiration – and that's just
Panorama.

**Will Carling in a motivational business
speech (1995)**

Bums Rush

I may not have been very tall or very athletic, but the one thing I did have was the most effective backside in world rugby.
Jim Glennon (1991)

On female rugby teams – Everybody thinks we should have moustaches and hairy arses, but in fact you could put us all on the cover of *Vogue*.
Helen Kirk (1987)

As Erica Roe streaked at Twickenham – Bill, there's a guy just run on the park with your backside on his chest.
Steve Smith (1982)

The lads say my bum is the equivalent of one 'Erica'.
Bill Beaumont

Bestiality

Summing up during the 'Dolphin hooks penis round man's leg' indecent sexual act court case – Men do not greet one another like this ... except perhaps at rugby club dinners.
Alan Cooper's Defence Counsel (1991)

On renaming Bradford Northern as the Bulls – Bradford is famous for sheep, but we didn't think that had quite the same ring. When we asked on local radio for a name with Yorkshire connotations someone suggested puddings. So it's Bulls.
Peter Deakin (1995)

(N.B. The new club magazine is called *Bullsheet*)

Codes A Nostra

League is much, much more physical than Union, and that's before anyone starts breaking the rules.
Adrian Hadley (1988)

The main difference between playing League and Union is that now I get my hangovers on Monday instead of Sunday.
Tom David

Anyone who doesn't watch rugby league is not a real person. He's a cow's hoof, an ethnic or comes from Melbourne.
John Singleton *Australian* (1981)

Anyone who's seen the Wigan [League] players stripped has been faced with the raw truth of the matter ... No time for male modelling, and even Princess Di would think twice about getting too close to that lot.
Colin Welland *The Observer* (1995)

On yet another Union defection to League – It's not Terry Holmes that Bradford Northern need – it's Sherlock!
Alex Murphy (1985)

Gareth Edwards: The sooner that little so-and-so goes to rugby league, the better it will be for us.
Dickie Jeeps (1967)

On the biggest change after returning to the Union code – It's the first time I've been cold for seven years. I was never cold playing rugby league.
Jonathan Davies *A Question of Sport* **BBC TV (1995)**

I'm 49, I've had a brain haemorrhage and a triple bypass and I could still go out and play a reasonable game of rugby union. But I wouldn't last 30 seconds in rugby league.
Graham Lowe (1995)

Cross Selection

On England's new look against Australia – This looks a good team on paper, let's see how it looks on grass.
Nigel Melville (1984)

On his son Huw's choice to play for England – I knew he would never play for Wales ... he's tone deaf.
Vernon Davies (1981)

The French selectors never do anything by halves; for the first international of the season against Ireland they dropped half the three-quarter line.
Nigel Starmer-Smith, BBC TV (1974)

Ear, Nose And Throat

I prefer rugby to soccer. I enjoy the violence in rugby, except when they start biting each other's ears off.
Elizabeth Taylor (1972)

After biting Sean Fitzpatrick's ear – For an 18-month suspension, I feel I probably should have torn it off. Then at least I could say, 'Look, I've returned to South Africa with the guy's ear.'
Johan le Roux (1994)

I think Brian Moore's gnashers are the kind you get from a DIY shop and hammer in yourself. He is the only player we have who looks like a French forward.
Paul Rendall (1994)

Fission Tackle

On trying to stop Phil Horrocks-Taylor – Every time I went to tackle him, Horrocks went one way, Taylor went the other, and all I got was the bloody hyphen.
Nick England

You've got to get your first tackle in early, even if it's late.
Ray Gravell

Food And Drink

Ray Gravell Eats Soft Centres.
Banner at Cardiff Arms Park (1970s)

I can't even spell 'diet'.
Gareth Edwards (1984)

On playing his last game of rugby for Bath – I thought I would have a quiet pint ... and about 17 noisy ones.
Gareth Chilcott (1993)

The Holy Writ of Gloucester Rugby Club demands: first, that the forwards shall win the ball; second, that the forwards shall keep the ball; and third, the backs shall buy the beer.

Doug Ibbotson

Rugby is not like tea, which is good only in England, with English water and English milk. On the contrary, rugby would be better, frankly, if it were made in a Twickenham pot and warmed up in a Pyrenean cauldron.

Dennis LaLanne (1960)

Forward Momentum

Forwards are the gnarled and scarred creatures who have a propensity for running into and bleeding all over each other.

Peter Fitzsimmons *Rugby Stories* **(1993)**

A forward's usefulness to his side varies as to the square of his distance from the ball.

Clarrie Gibbons

I don't know why prop forwards play rugby.

Lionel Weston (1974)

The one-handed palmer can always reach higher, they say. They may be right, but the result is that nearly every line-out is like a tropical island – all waving palms.

Vivian Jenkins

In 1823, William Webb Ellis first picked up the ball in his arms and ran with it. And for the next 156 years forwards have been trying to work out why.

Sir Tasker Watkins (1979)

Colin Meads is the kind of player you expect to see emerging from a ruck with the remains of a jockstrap between his teeth.

Tom O'Reilly

Wade Dooley: With a handle like that he sounds more like a western sheriff than the Lancashire bobby that he is.

Norman Mair *The Scotsman* **(1988)**

Dean Richards is nicknamed Warren, as in warren ugly bastard.

Jason Leonard (1995)

Condom Is Back In French Pack.

Independent headline

On the Munster pack – Mothers keep their photo on the mantelpiece to stop the kids going too near the fire.

Jim Neilly, BBC TV (1995)

Full Backs

After JPR Williams was involved in a road traffic accident – Bloody typical, isn't it! The car's a write-off. The tanker's a write-off. But JPR comes out of it all in one piece.

Gareth Edwards (1978)

Bob Hillier had the hair of a city slicker and the hoofing toecap of a Tunisian mule.

Frank Keating

Injuries

On his multi-player injury substitutions against Western Samoa – It was like the Falklands crisis. I was counting them in and counting them out.

Jack Rowell (1995)

After a succession of career-threatening injuries – I played ten injury-free years between the ages of 12 and 22. Then, suddenly, it seemed like I was allergic to the twentieth century.

Nigel Melville (1984)

In my time, I've had my knee out, broken my collarbone, had my nose smashed, a rib broken, lost a few teeth, and ricked my back; but as soon as I get a bit of bad luck I'm going to quit the game.

J. W. Robinson

New Zealand rugby is a colourful game since you get all black ... and blue.

Anon

Irish Stew

Old soldiers do not fade away from the Irish team. They make comebacks.

Anon Dublin sportswriter

On playing for Wales at Lansdowne Road, Dublin – I didn't know what was going on at the start in the swirling wind. The flags were all pointing in different directions and I thought the Irish had starched them just to fool us.

Mike Watkins (1984)

Tony Ward is the most important rugby player in Ireland. His legs are far more important to his country than even those of Marlene Dietrich were to the film industry. A little hairier, maybe, but a pair of absolute winners.

C.M.H. Gibson, Wales v Ireland match programme (1979)

Land Of My Fathers

Don't ask me about emotions in the Welsh dressing room. I'm someone who cries when he watches *Little House on the Prairie*.

Robert Norster (1994)

On Wales losing 28–9 against Australia – No leadership, no ideas. Not even enough imagination to thump someone in the line-up when the ref wasn't looking.

J.P.R. Williams (1984)

We've lost seven of our last eight matches. Only team that we've beaten was Western Samoa. Good job we didn't play the whole of Samoa.

Gareth Davies (1989)

The job of Welsh coach is like a minor part in a Quentin Tarantino film: you stagger on, you hallucinate, nobody seems to understand a word you say, you throw up, you get shot. Poor old Kevin Bowring has come up through the coaching structure so he knows what it takes ... 15 more players than Wales have at present.

Mark Reason *Total Sport* **(1996)**

League Of Their Own

To play rugby league, you need three things: a good pass, a good tackle and a good excuse.

Anon

In south west Lancashire, babes don't toddle, they side-step. Queuing women talk of 'nipping round the blindside'. Rugby league provides our cultural adrenalin. It's a physical manifestation of our rules of life, comradeship, honest endeavour, and a staunch, often ponderous allegiance to fair play.

Colin Welland (1979)

Load Of Balls

Rugby is played by men with odd shaped balls.

Car bumper sticker

Rugby is a game for the mentally deficient ... That is why it was invented by the British. Who else but an Englishman could invent an oval ball?

Peter Pook *Pook's Love Nest*

There is far too much talk about good ball and bad ball. In my opinion, good ball is when you have possession and bad ball is when the opposition have it.

Dick Jeeps (1976)

Name Game

After John Jeffrey had 'dropped and badly damaged' the Calcutta Cup – It will now have to be called the Calcutta Shield.

Bob Munro (1988)

On taking over as Batley chairman – Not many people in Batley speak Latin, so the first thing we did was change the motto.

Stephen Ball (1989)

Officially Speaking

The advantage law is the best law in rugby, because it lets you ignore all the others for the good of the game.

Derek Robinson

The first half is invariably much longer than the second. This is partly because of the late kick-off but is also caused by the unfitness of the referee.

Michael Green *The Art of Coarse Rugby* **(1960)**

I think you enjoy the game more if you don't know the rules. Anyway, you're on the same wavelength as the referees.

Jonathan Davies, *A Question of Sport* **BBC TV (1995)**

Rite Result

When it comes to the one great scorer,
To mark against your name.
He'll not ask how you played the game,
But ... whether you beat England!

Max Boyce

Rugby is picking the ball from the back
of the scrum in 1974 and scoring a try
against Wales at Twickenham and
realising 'I sort of hit it and it was in the
back of the net, Brian' is fairly
appropriate.

Andy Ripley

Root Of All Evil

I'm still an amateur, of course, but I
became rugby's first millionaire five
years ago.

David Campese (1991)

To Princess Anne's son Peter Phillips,
Gordonstoun School's rugby captain, for
his pre-match coin-toss preference –
Grandmother or tails, sir?

Anon rugby referee (1995)

On the smaller Union clubs not going
professional – No one has ever
suggested that the likes of Old Rubber
Duckians should start paying their guys
for playing.

Brian Moore (1996)

School Terms

Playing rugby at school I once fell on a
loose ball and, through ignorance and
fear, held on despite a fierce
pummelling. After that it took me
months to convince my team-mates I
was a coward.

Peter Cook (1970)

A major rugby tour by the British Isles to
New Zealand is a cross between a
medieval crusade and a prep school
outing.

John Hopkins

Swing Lomu

On Jonah Lomu – There's no doubt
about it, he's a big bastard.

Gavin Hastings (1995)

On Jonah Lomu – I've seen a lot people
like him, but they weren't playing on the
wing.

Colin Meads (1995)

On Jonah Lomu – The Brent Spar with
attitude. A figure who inspires hero
worship among even those who think a
fly-half is a glass of beer consumed
when 'er indoors is looking the other
way.

Robert Philip *Daily Telegraph* **(1995)**

Before the New Zealand v England
World Cup semi-final – Remember that
rugby is a team game; all 14 of you make
sure you pass the ball to Jonah.

Anon fax to N.Z. team (1995)

Me? As England's answer to Jonah Lomu? Joanna Lumley, more likely.
Damian Hopley (1995)

On Lomu finally turning down offers from League teams – Jonah Lomu is staying in New Zealand, ending an is-he-or-isn't-he saga which rivalled the trial of O.J. Simpson for unnecessarily protracted tedium.
Paul Wilson *The Observer* **(1995)**

Vitriol And Violence

Rugby football is a game I can't claim absolutely to understand in all its niceties, if you know what I mean. I can follow the broad, general principles, of course. I mean to say, I know that the main scheme is to work the ball down the field somehow and deposit it over the line at the other end and that, in order to squalch this programme, each side is allowed to put in a certain amount of assault and battery and do things to its fellow man which, if done elsewhere, would result in 14 days without the option, coupled with some strong remarks from the Bench.
P. G. Wodehouse *Very Good, Jeeves* **(1930)**

Following the infamous soccer kung-fu kick – Playing the French is like facing 15 Eric Cantonas. They are brilliant but brutal.
Brian Moore (1995)

Following Scotland's accusations of French foul play – If you can't take a punch, you should play table tennis.
Pierre Berbizier (1995)

Welcome In The Hills

Pre-game pep talk before facing England – Look what these bastards have done to Wales. They've taken our coal, our water, our steel. They buy our houses and they only live in them for a fortnight every 12 months. What have they given us? Absolutely nothing. We've been exploited, raped, controlled and punished by the English – and that's who you are playing this afternoon.
Phil Bennett (1977)

The relationship between the Welsh and the English is based on trust and understanding. They don't trust us and we don't understand them.
Dudley Wood (1986)

MONICA SELES HAS SO MUCH CONTROL OF THE RACKET WITH THOSE DOUBLE-HANDED WRISTS.

Virginia Wade, BBC TV

Comedy Of Eras

Andre Agassi was recently born again. Now, if he can only grow up.

***Sports Illustrated* (1989)**

On John McEnroe – I don't know that my behaviour has improved that much with age. They just found someone worse.

Jimmy Connors (1984)

On why she turned pro while still at school – I hate homework.

Maureen 'Peanut' Louie

Tennis is a young man's game. Until you're 25, you can play singles. From 25 to 35, you should play doubles. I won't tell you exactly how old I am, but when I played, there were 28 men on the court – just on my side of the net.

George Burns

When I was 40 my doctor advised me that a man in his forties shouldn't play tennis. I heeded his advice carefully and could hardly wait until I reached 50 to start again.

Hugo L. Black

Defeated and Deflated

If you don't do something special against Chris Evert you find yourself losing concentration after 35 shots.
Julie Heldman (1972)

John McEnroe's so good. Against him, all you can do is shake hands and take a shower.
Tomas Smid (1984)

On losing badly to McEnroe at Wimbledon – For two weeks I've been seeing the ball like a basketball. Today, I couldn't see it.
Jimmy Connors (1984)

On what she had learned after a number of quick losses to Martina Navratilova – How to shake hands.
Bettina Bunge

Different Ball Game

Tennis players are a load of w**kers. I'd love to put John McEnroe in the centre for Fulham [Rugby League Club] and let some of the big players sort him out.
Colin Welland (1980)

Martina's like the old Green Bay Packers. You know exactly what she's going to do, but there isn't a thing you can do about it.
Arthur Ashe

The tennis star is insulting because the pampered little sh*t has never had his ass kicked by a middle linebacker.
Dan Jenkins *Playboy* (1985)

Double Trouble

The best doubles pair in the world is John McEnroe and anyone else.
Peter Fleming (1990)

On winning his first singles tournament for a decade, having won many doubles titles with his twin brother Tim – It was nice to stand in the winner's circle and not have to share 50 per cent of the money with my brother.

Tom Gullikson (1985)

Fashion Statement

Tennis was a game invented by a woman named Samantha Tennis in 1839, in the village of Lobsworth, County of Kent, as a diversion for the wealthy and titled Englishmen of the region, who had nothing better to do at the time but drink, belch and wear funny clothes.

Dan Jenkins *What Is It?*

On Martina Navratilova's new line in court clothing – She's become a Slav to fashion.

Kim Cunningham

On Stan Smith's personalised Adidas footwear – Dad, did they name the shoe after you, or were you named after the shoe?

Trevor Smith

Food And Drink

I think Pete Sampras has really reached his peak. About the only thing he doesn't do is cook.

Michael Chang (1994)

After being asked if he had ever played in New Jersey – I must have. I remember the bar across the street.

Rod Laver

Listening to Britons dining out is like watching people play first-class tennis with imaginary balls.

Margaret Halsey

On retiring early – Being a champion is all well and good, but you can't eat a crown.

Althea Gibson

I'm Mobile

Arantxa Sanchez-Vicario bustled this way and that, as if mounted on castors and hurtling across a highly polished floor.

Rex Bellamy *The Times* **(1989)**

Charlie Pasarell moves so slowly between points, that at times he seems to be flirting with reverse gear.

Rex Bellamy *The Times*

Keeping Up Appearances

Bjorn Borg looks like a hunchbacked, jut-bottomed version of Lizabeth Scott, impersonating a bearded Apache princess.

Clive James

John McEnroe has hair like badly turned broccoli.

Clive James *The Observer*

John McEnroe looks as if he is serving round the edge of an imaginary building.

Clive James *The Observer*

Not since Betty Grable has so much been written about a pair of legs as John Lloyd's. Nastase's agent told me, in a fit of jealousy, that he hopes Lloyd gets varicose veins.

Taki (1978)

Ivan Lendl is a robot, a solitary, mechanical man who lives with his dogs behind towering walls at his estate in Connecticut. A man who so badly wants to have a more human image that he's having surgery to remove the bolts from his neck.

Tony Kornheiser *Washington Post*

Jim Courier – that pneumatic Charlie Brown.

Allison Pearson *Independent on Sunday* **(1994)**

Ladies Sin Girls

At Wimbledon, the ladies are simply the candles on the cake.
John Newcombe

If someone says tennis is not feminine, I say screw it.
Rosie Casals

I may have exaggerated a bit when I said that 80 per cent of the top women tennis players are fat pigs. It's only 75 per cent.
Richard Krajicek (1992)

Hardy Amies once told me that the sexiest thing he had seen was nuns playing tennis.
Prudence Glynn *The Observer* **(1981)**

Mixed Reception

In lawn tennis mixed, the basic chivalry move is to pretend to serve less fiercely to the woman than to the man. This is particularly useful if your first service tends to be out in any case.
Stephen Potter *Lifemanship*

You can almost watch a couple play mixed doubles and know whether they should stay together.
Dr Herbert Hendin

Mixed doubles are always starting divorces. If you play with your wife, you fight with her; if you play with somebody else, she fights with you.
Sidney Wood

The proper method of playing mixed doubles is to swipe the ball accidentally and straight at the woman opponent as hard and as accurately as possible. Male players must not only retain equanimity on their side of the net, but create dissension on the other.
Art Hoppe

An otherwise happily married couple may turn a mixed doubles game into a scene from *Who's Afraid of Virginia Woolf.*
Rod Laver

Motor Vation

Andrea Jaeger plays tennis like she's double-parked.
Mary Carillo

On Steffi Graf's first round defeat at Wimbledon by Lori McNeil – Steffi Grief ... the unstoppable juggernaut of women's tennis has just been run over by a Lori.
The Sun **(1994)**

After beating 14-year-old Jennifer Capriati to win a car – It's just as well that I won, because if Jennifer won, she couldn't drive it anyway.
Martina Navratilova

Like a Volvo, Bjorn Borg is rugged, has good after-sales service, and is very dull.
Clive James *The Observer*

Bjoring Borg ... a Volvo among tennis stars.
Peter Freedman *Glad to be Grey* **(1985)**

Name Game

If Borg's parents hadn't liked the name, he might never have been Bjorn.
Marty Indik

Everyone thinks my name is Jerry Laitis and they call me Mr Laitis. What can you do when you have a name that sounds like a disease?
Vitas Gerulaitis (1977)

Arantxa Sanchez-Vicario is the only sports person whose name is worth 175 in Scrabble.
Nick Hancock *They Think It's All Over* **BBC TV (1995)**

One-Dimensional

Ivan Lendl's never going to be a great player on grass. The only time he comes to the net is to shake your hand.
Goran Ivanisevic (1992)

Taut and tight-lipped mistress of the baseline, Chris Evert is the all-American golden girl become the champion of monotony.
Paul West

Power Play

Jimmy Connors likes the ball to come at him in a straight line, so that he can hit it back in another straight line. When it comes to him in a curve, he uses up half of his energy straightening it up again.
Clive James

I can't believe how hard Agassi hits the ball. It's like he's got a gun. No one hit the ball like that in my day. Ion Tiriac didn't drive that fast.

Ilie Nastase (1988)

Service Included

The serve was invented so that the net could play.

Bill Cosby

Roscoe Tanner seems to have found a way of making his service go even faster, so that the ball is now quite invisible, like Stealth, the American supersonic bomber which nobody has ever seen.

Clive James *The Observer* **(1981)**

Though your game is hardly the best
You can fray your opponent's nerves
By methodically bouncing the ball
At least ten times before your serves.

Arnold J. Zarett

Super Brat

McEnroe claims John Lloyd is more popular than him because Lloyd married Chris Evert. McEnroe wouldn't be popular if he was married to Marie Osmond.

Terry Kelleher (1979)

Professionalism in tennis ... only resulted in making billionaires out of rude children, producing an onslaught of moody defectors, and a lot of guys with hair that looks as if bats slept in it ... Meanwhile, my head swims with the thought that I have watched tennis progress from Don Budge and Alice Marble to Farrah Fawcett becoming John McEnroe's mother-in-law.

Dan Jenkins *Playboy* **(1985)**

I'm an American. You can't go on where you were born. If you do then John McEnroe would be a German.

Martina Navratilova

On making the semi-finals of the Australian Open – It's just like you expected – Edberg, Lendl, McEnroe, and Becker.

Patrick McEnroe

Technique

I have finally mastered what to do with the second tennis ball. Having small hands, I was becoming terribly self-conscious about keeping it in a can in the car while I served the first one. I noted some women tucked the second ball just inside the elastic leg of their tennis panties. I tried, but found the space already occupied by a leg. Now, I simply drop the second ball down my cleavage, giving me a chest that often stuns my opponent throughout an entire set.

Erma Brombeck *If Life is a Bowl of Cherries ...* **(1978)**

My theory is that if you buy an ice-cream cone and make it hit your mouth, you can play. If you stick it on your forehead, your chances are less.

Vic Braden

I don't think I've ever held a racket in my hand ... There's got to be somebody in the US who isn't trying to play tennis and stinking up the court.

Isaac Asimov

Good shot, bad luck and hell are the five basic words to be used in tennis.

Virginia Graham

True Brit

Ten of the world's greatest rarities: No. 4: A British tennis player with a can of silver polish.

Journalists *Mail on Sunday*

On Canadian Greg Rusedski becoming British number one – I get a kick out of watching him pick up the accent. He's using words such as 'brilliant' and 'lovely'.

Andre Agassi (1995)

Upset Point

The Benson and Hedges Cup was won by McEnroe ... he was as charming as always, which means that he was as charming as a dead mouse in a loaf of bread.

Clive James *The Observer* **(1980)**

On being told to address Ilie Nastase as Mister – Look, Nastase, we used to have a famous cricket match in this country called Gentlemen versus Players. The Gentlemen were put down on the scorecard as 'Mister' because they were gentlemen. By no stretch of the imagination can anybody call you a gentleman.

Trader Horn, Wimbledon umpire

Nastase is a Hamlet who wants to play a clown. He is no good at it ... Nastase rarely grins and bears it. More commonly he grins, groans, shrugs, slumps, spins around, shakes his head, puffs out his cheeks, rolls on the ground and bears it. Even more common, he does all that and doesn't bear it.

Clive James *The Observer*

On being Nastase's coach – I feel like dog trainer who teach dog manners and graces and just when you think dog knows how should act with nice qualities, dog make big puddle and all is wasted.

Ion Tiriac (1972)

After being fined $70,000 – Team Tennis wanted a circus, so I gave them a circus.

Ilie Nastase

The crowds at Flushing Meadow are about as impartial as a Nuremberg Rally.

Ian Wooldridge *Daily Mail* **(1995)**

Wimbledon

A traditional fixture at Wimbledon is the way the BBC TV commentary box fills up with British players eliminated in the early rounds.
Clive James *The Observer* **(1981)**

The one foolproof way of putting the ticket touts out of business – a Wimbledon final between Pete Sampras and Jim Courier.
The Guardian **(1993)**

I often surprise myself. You can't plan some shots that go in, not unless you're on marijuana, and the only grass I'm partial to is Wimbledon's.
Rod Laver (1970)

On the traditional English summer – It's always the same. Either it's rainy with sunny intervals or sunny with rainy intervals.
Pat DuPre

Wimbledon is getting a bit too like Royal Ascot. It's not what happens or who wins so much, as what clothes do I have on.
David Lloyd (1995)

Winning And Losing

Why did I lose? No reason, though you might like to know that I got tired, my ears started popping, the rubber came off my shoes, I got cramp, and I lost one of my contact lenses. Other than that I was in great shape.
Bob Lutz (1976)

When Ilie Nastase's winning he's objectionable. When he's losing, he's highly objectionable.
Adrian Clark

After losing to Ivan Lendl in under an hour – Sure, on a given day I could beat him. But it would have to be a day he had food poisoning.
Mel Purcell

After an early singles exit at Wimbledon – All that's left for me to do is go find John Lloyd and start a family.
Pam Shriver (1986)

After struggling to beat Hu Na – You figure there's eight trillion people in China, and if she's number one there, it says something.
Pam Shriver

DO IT ... BUMPER STICKERS

Backstrokers do it without getting their face wet
Baseball players do it at home
Divers do it deeper than anyone else
Fencers always do it with protection
Gliders do it and can keep it up all day
Goal-keepers never do it near the other half
Golfers do it best when they are below par
Hang-gliders do it on their own
Shot putters do it on one leg
Skiers do it with their legs together
Skiers do it on the piste
Skiers go down faster
Snooker players do it bending over a table
Squash players do it against the wall
Swimmers do it with the breaststroke
Tennis players start with love
Ten-pin bowlers do it with something to spare
Torvill and Dean do it on thin ice
Water-skiers do it in rubber suits
Windsurfers do it standing up

"United Sports of America"

If Don Mattingly isn't the American League Most Valuable Player, nothing in China is kosher.

**Phil Rizzuto,
New York Yankees game announcer**

Bad News Bearers

After announcing the death of Pope Paul VI – Well, that kind of puts the damper on even a Yankees win.

Phil Rizzuto

Things were so bad in Chicago last summer, that by the fifth inning the White Sox were selling hot dogs to go.

Ken Brett (1977)

On being asked to take a pay cut from $20,000 to $7,500 – Tell you what, you keep the salary and I'll keep me the cut.

Vernon 'Lefty' Gomez

The Houston Astros play in a vast indoor stadium known as the Astrodome, but the problem is they field a half-vast team.

Kurt Bevacqua

On the inconsistent San Diego Padres – One night we play like King Kong, the next night like Fay Wray.

Terry Kennedy

They've played on grass and they've played on Astroturf. What they should do is put down a layer of paper in Candlestick Park. After all, the Giants always look good on paper.

Don Rose

The only good thing about playing for Cleveland is you don't have to make road trips there.

Richie Scheinblum

Field Of Dreams

Claudell Washington plays the outfield like he's trying to catch grenades.
Reggie Jackson

There is nothing remarkable about throwing or catching or hitting a ball. Jugglers in Yugoslavia do it better.
Jim Murray *Los Angeles Times* **(1974)**

Let's see who we have on the bags. We have Who's on first, What's on second, I Don't Know's on third.
Bud Abbott and Lou Costello *Who's on First ... ?*

The Front Office

Managing a baseball team is like trying to make chicken salad out of chicken sh*t.
Joe Kuhel

The secret of managing a ball club is to keep the five guys who hate you away from the five who are undecided.
Charles 'Casey' Stengel

Football coaches walk across the field after the game and pretend to congratulate the opposing coach. Baseball managers head right for the beer.
Thomas Boswell *Washington Post*

Yankees' owner George Steinbrenner is a first-and-ten capitalist in a bunt-and-run world.
Tom Boswell

It's a good thing 'Babe' Ruth isn't still with the Yankees. If he was, George Steinbrenner would have him bat seventh and say he's overweight.
Graig Nettles

Name Dropping

When you say you're a padre, people ask when did you become a parent. When you say you're a cardinal, they tell you to work hard because the next step is pope. But when you say you're a Dodger, everybody knows you're in the Major Leagues.
Tommy LaSorda

Orel Hershiser is the only Major League pitcher to have two consecutive pronouns in his surname.
Roger Angell

Fernando Valenzuela is the pitcher whose name sounds like a mailing address in the Lower Andes.
Tom Boswell

On the appearance of Clayton Moore at a Blue Jays home game – It's not very often you get to see the Lone Ranger and Toronto in the same night.
Bobby Bragan

After being traded and retraded by the Red Sox to the White Sox and back – I find that every five years a man has to change his Sox.
Steve Lyons

Officially Speaking

Many fans look upon an umpire as a necessary evil to the luxury of baseball, like the odour that follows an automobile.

Christy Matthewson

They expect an umpire to be perfect on opening day and to improve as the season goes on.

Nestor Chylak

In a way, an umpire is like a woman. He makes quick decisions, never reverses them, and doesn't think you're safe when you're out.

Larry Goetz

I sometimes get birthday cards from fans. But it's often the same message – they hope it's my last.

Al Norman

On having his eyesight called into question – I can see the sun okay, and that's 93 million miles away.

Bruce Froemming (1987)

Pitch Black

Throw strikes – home plate don't move.

Leroy 'Satchel' Paige

The way to *catch* a knuckleball is to wait until the ball has stopped rolling and then pick it up.

Bob Uecker

Throwing a fast ball by Hank Aaron is like trying to sneak the sunrise past a rooster.

Curt Simmons

Robert 'Lefty' Grove could throw a lamb chop past a wolf.

Arthur 'Bugs' Baer

Arthur 'Dazzy' Vance could throw a cream puff through a battleship.

Johnny Frederick

Nolan Ryan is baseball's exorcist – he scares the devil out of you.

Dick Sharon

We've got a problem here. Luis Tiant wants to use the bathroom, and it says no foreign objects in the toilets.

Graig Nettles

Players

There are two kinds of ball-players – prospects and suspects. And the suspects don't like the prospects.

Anon

Baseball is the favourite American sport because it's so slow. Any idiot can follow it. And just about any idiot can play it.

Gore Vidal

[American] Football isn't some sport where you play 8,000 games and run out to second base and call time because you've got a hangnail.

Norm Van Brocklin

Baseball is the only game left for people. To play basketball, you have to be 7 feet 6 inches. To play football, you have to be the same width.
Bill Veeck (1975)

Baseball players are smarter than [American] football players. How often do you see a baseball team penalised for too many men on the pitch?
Jim Bouton

Kevin Mitchell found God in Spring training. Then every night he tried to find a goddess.
Lennie Dykstra

Running Sacred

Baseball is a game which consists of tapping a ball with a piece of wood, then running like a lunatic.
H. J. Dutiel

James 'Cool Papa' Bell was so fast, one time he hit a line drive right back past my ear. I turned round and saw the ball hit his ass sliding into second.
Leroy 'Satchel' Paige

Bruce Benedict is so slow he'd finish third in a race with a pregnant woman.
Tommy LaSorda

Smash Hits

As far as John Kruk is concerned, it ain't over till the fat guy swings.
Darren Daulton

Harmon Killebrew has enough power to hit home runs in any park – including Yellowstone.
Paul Richards

Stan Musial could hit .300 with a fountain pen.
Joe Garagiola

You've got to swing that bat; only the mailman walks.
Kevin 'The Mailman' Mitchell (1989)

When Neil Armstrong first set foot on the moon, he and all the space scientists were puzzled by an unidentifiable white object. I knew immediately what it was. That was a home run hit off me in 1937 by Jimmy Foxx.
Vernon 'Lefty' Gomez

George 'Babe' Ruth and Old Jack Dempsey, both Sultans of Swat,
One hits where the other people are, the other where they're not.
John Lardner

Struck Out Swinging

Call me Un-American; call me Canadian or Swedish, I don't care. I hate baseball ... I have lots of reasons to hate baseball. For one it's dull. Nothing happens. Watching baseball is like going to a lecture by a member of the Slow ... Talkers ... of ... America. It's like turning on the TV – when the cable is out. It's like watching grass – no, Astroturf grow.
Jeff Jarvis *Entertainment Weekly* (1990)

Hating the New York Yankees is as American as apple pie, unwed mothers and cheating on your income tax.
Mike Royko (1981)

The underprivileged people of the Americas play some strange game with a bat which looks like an overgrown rolling pin.
Fred Trueman

I don't think I can be expected to take seriously a game which takes less than three days to reach its conclusion.
Tom Stoppard (1984)

You remember baseball? A sort of razzamatazz rounders, played by rowdy roughnecks, wielding oversize clubs and oversized tennis balls.
Robert Steen

Vital Organs

You have only two hemispheres in your brain – a left and a right side. The left side controls the right side of your body and the right controls the left half. It's a fact. Therefore, left-handers are the only people in their right minds.
Bill 'The Spaceman' Lee

When Athletics' owner Charlie Finley had his heart operation, it took eight hours – seven and a half to find his heart.
Steve McCatty

Baseball without fans is like Jayne Mansfield without a sweater. Hang on, that can be taken two ways.
Richard Nixon

Win, Lose Or ...

There's three things you can do in a baseball game – you can win, you can lose, or it can rain.
Charles 'Casey' Stengel

The key to winning baseball games is pitching, fundamentals and three-run homers.
Earl Weaver

When you win you eat better, sleep better and your beer tastes better. And your wife looks like Gina Lollobrigida.
Johnny Pesky

World Serious

Calling it the World Series must impress the world as an example of America's modesty.
Anon

On playing against a team from Japan – An hour after the game, you want to go out and play them again.
Rocky Bridges

On playing in Japan – It was strange. The only English words I saw were Sony and Mitsubishi.
Bill Gullickson

Detroit fans don't know anything about baseball. They couldn't tell the difference between baseball players and Japanese aviators.
Mayo Smith

NEVER SAY DIE

Old archers never die, they simply bow out.
Colin M. Jarman

Old bowls players never die, they simply jack it in.
Colin M. Jarman

Old card-players never die, they simply shuffle off.
Felicia DeMartin

Old chess players never die, they simply go to pieces.
Colin M. Jarman

Old croquet players never die, they simply peg out.
Anon

Old fishermen never die, they simply smell that way.
Anon

Old golfers never die, they simply lose their drive.
Anon

Old golfers don't die, we just lose our distance.
Ralph Gudahl

Old golfers never die, they simply putter away.
Colin M. Jarman

Old mountaineers never die, they simply lose their grip.
Colin M. Jarman

Old on-course bookmakers never die, they simply go off the rails.
Colin M. Jarman

Old rugby players never die, they simply have their balls taken away.
Anon

Old rugby players never die, they just pass away.
Craig Fleishman

Old shot-putters never die, they just get weak.
Otis Chandler

Old skaters never die, they just lose their ice sight.
Anon

Old ski-jumpers never die, they simply lose their inclination.
Colin M. Jarman

Old snooker players never die, they simply go to pot.
Colin M. Jarman

Old tennis players never die, they are simply put out to grass.
Anon

Old tobogannists never die, they are simply deluged.
Colin M. Jarman

Old yachtsmen never die, they simply keel over.
Colin M. Jarman

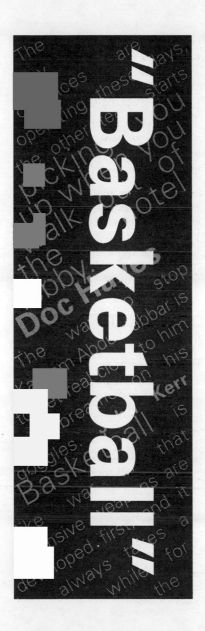

"Basketball"

Coaching Ins And Outs

When the list of great coaches is finally read out, I believe Frank Layden will be there … listening.

Pat Williams

Defence Of The Realm

The way defences are operating these days, the other team starts picking you up when you walk out of the hotel lobby.

Doc Hayes

The way to stop Kareem Abdul-Jabbar is to get real close to him and breathe on his goggles.

John Kerr

Basketball is like war in that offensive weapons are developed first, and it always takes a while for the defence to catch up.

Red Auerbach

On his Belmar New Jersey Girls' High School tactics – We play a *man-to-man* defence. Person to person sounds like a telephone call

Anon Coach (1982)

Learning Curve

I'm in favour of drug tests, just so long as they are multiple choice.

Kurt Rambis

On his academic aspirations – The only way I can make five As is when I sign my name.
Alaa Adbelnaby

I believe in higher education. You know, 6'8", 6'9", 6'10".
David Gaines

Fan To See Basketball

On his Washington State college team – Fans never fall asleep at our games because they're afraid they might get hit with a pass.
George Raveling

This is the second most exciting indoor sport, and the other one shouldn't have spectators.
Dick Vertlieb

Illness And Injury

On his 916th game as coach at University of Alabama – I've been here so long that when I got here the Dead Sea wasn't even sick.
Wimp Sanderson

I learned a long time ago that minor surgery is when they do the operation on someone else, not you.
Bill Walton

Bill Walton is incredible. If you drop a toothpick on his foot, he'll have a stress fracture.
Stan Albeck

I sight down my nose to shoot, and now my nose isn't straight since I broke it. That's why my shooting has been off.
Barrie Haynie

I told Zollie Volchok [Sonics general manager] we needed an ultrasound machine and he asked me why we needed music in the locker room.
Lennie Wilkens

On his homesickness during the Barcelona Olympics – I miss America. I miss crime and murder. I miss Philadelphia. There hasn't been a brutal stabbing or anything here the last 24 hours. I've missed it.
Charles Barkley (1992)

Jordanian Air Lines

There are some remarkable parallels between basketball and politics. Michael Jordan has already mastered the skill most needed for political success: how to stay aloft without visible means of support.
Margaret Thatcher (1992)

After Michael Jordan had scored a play-off record 69 points – I'll always remember this as the night Michael and I combined to score 70 points.
Stacey King

On the seemingly one-sided relationship between Michael Jordan and his shoe sponsors Nike – The company should change its name to Mike.
Alvin Robertson

Magic Johnson is the best player who plays on the ground, and Michael Jordan is the best player who plays in the air.
John Paxson

In my prime I could have handled Michael Jordan. Of course, he would be only 12 years old.
Jerry Sloan

You don't hesitate with Michael, or you'll end up on some poster in a gift shop someplace.
Felton Spencer

Officially Speaking

You can say something to popes, kings and presidents, but you can't talk to officials. In the next war they ought to give everyone a whistle.
Abe Lemmons (1977)

On females officiating in the NBA – Incompetence should not be confined to one sex.
Bill Russell (1976)

The trouble with officials is they just don't care who wins.
Tommy Canterbury

Players

To say a good defensive centre is more important than a high-scoring forward is like saying that the intestinal tract is more vital than the circulatory system.
Telford Taylor *New York Times* (1979)

The way my team are doing, we could get Wilt Chamberlain in a trade and find out that he's really two midgets Scotch-taped together.
Gene Shue (1967)

Here's a six-foot-ten guy in sneakers and the lady's asking me, 'Profession?'
Jack McMahon (1965)
(Elvin Hayes had a stock reply to this line of enquiry: 'I clean giraffe ears.')

George McGinnis has got the body of a Greek god and the running ability of a Greek goddess.
Dick Vitale

On Atlanta's proposed Dominique Wilkins Freeway – That's the one with all the 'No Passing' signs.
Anon Atlanta disc jockey

I told one player, 'Son, I couldn't understand it with you. Is it ignorance or apathy?' He said, 'Coach, I don't know and I don't care.'
Frank Layden

If you can walk with your head in the clouds and keep your feet on the ground, you can make a million dollars in the NBA.
Gary Dornhoefer (1975)

After an earthquake in Los Angeles – The earth in LA moved more in one hour than Benoit Benjamin did all last season with the Clippers.
Peter Vecsey

We told Stanley Roberts to go on a water diet, and Lake Superior disappeared.

Pat Williams

Going into a game against Lew Alcindor [later Kareem Abdul-Jabbar] is like going into a knife fight and finding there's no blade in your handle.

Bill Fitch

On the best tactic when playing alongside Kareem Abdul-Jabbar – Just give him the ball.

Earvin 'Magic' Johnson

I only know how to play two ways: reckless and abandon.

Earvin 'Magic' Johnson

Giving 'Magic' the basketball is like giving Hitler an army, Jesse James a gang, or Genghis Khan a horse. Devastation. Havoc.

Jim Murray *Los Angeles Times*

When Xavier McDaniel plays against Orlando Wooldridge, it's a coach's dream – X v O.

Mychal Thompson

Shot Selection

I never thought I'd lead the NBA in rebounding, but I got a lot of help from my team-mates – they did a lot of missing.

Moses Malone

We have a bunch of outside shooters. Unfortunately, all of our games are indoors.

Weldon Drew

Shooting is just like toenails. They may fall off occasionally, but you know they'll always come back.

Charles Johnson (1977)

Slammed And Dunked

Basketball, a game which won't be fit for people until they set the basket umbilicus-high and return the giraffes to the zoo.

Ogden Nash

If cocaine were helium, the NBA would float away.

Art Rust

Many Americans follow pro basketball from November through June, for reasons that I found unexplainable, other than the fact that they were overly fascinated with soaring armpits.

Dan Jenkins *You Call It Sports* ... **(1989)**

If the NBA was on Channel 5 and a bunch of frogs were making love on Channel 4, I'd watch the frogs, even if they were coming in fuzzy.

Bobby Knight

On how to make the game more exciting – Eliminate the referees, raise the basket four feet, double the size of the basketball, limit the height of the players to 5 feet 9 inches, bring back the centre jump, allow taxi drivers in for free and allow the players to carry guns.

Al McGuire

Basketball has so much showboating you'd think it was invented by Jerome Kern.

Art Spander

The game is too long, the season is too long and the players are too long.

Jack Dolph (1973)

Tactics

In basketball, the first person to touch the ball shoots it. Either that or the coach carefully diagrams a set play and then the first player to touch it shoots it.

Gene Klein

On his Oklahoma college team – This year we plan to run and shoot. Next season we hope to run and score.

Billy Tubbs

Part of the charm of basketball lies in the fact that it's a simple game to understand. Players race up and down a fairly small area indoors and stuff the ball into a ring with Madonna's dress hanging on it.

Dan Jenkins *You Call It Sports ...* (1989)

On a 17-game Orlando Magic losing streak – We can't win at home and we can't win on the road. My problem as general manager is I can't think of another place to play.

Pat Williams (1992)

On his telepathic understanding with James Worthy – It's almost like we have ESPN.

Earvin 'Magic' Johnson

Teams

Coach Red Auerbach makes mistakes, the entire Boston Celtics team makes mistakes, but they can get away with it because they have the world's largest eraser in centre Bill Russell.

Pepper Wilson

The team is boring and lifeless. For over 20 years the Boston Celtics have stood for something. The only thing they stand for now is the anthem.

Bob Ryan *Boston Globe*

It's rumoured that a well-known New England newspaper is to sponsor a topless female basketball team – to be called the Boston Globes.

***Playboy* (1981)**

On coaching the Oklahoma State Penitentiary team – We lost some mighty good boys from last year because of paroles, but, crime being what it is, we've picked up some good ones since then, too.

Joe Kirkpatrick

The LA Lakers are so good they could run a fast break with a medicine ball.

Rich Donnelly

I call Los Angeles the city of alternatives. If you don't like mountains, we got the ocean. If you don't like Knott's Berry Farm, we've got Disneyland. If you don't like basketball, we've got the Clippers.

Arsenio Hall

The Orlando Magic were so bad last season, the cheerleaders stayed home and phoned in their cheers.

Pat Williams

The Atlanta Hawks are a bunch of guys who would prefer to pass kidney stones than pass a basketball.

Bob Weiss

When I told my wife UConn would win the Big East tournament, she wanted to know why a team from Alaska got into the Big East tournament.

Vic Ziegel

After a heavy reverse – It was an 'AW' game. We were AWful and they were AWesome.

Anon NBA coach (1981)

My whole family likes to play basketball. George II plays for his high school team and George III and George IV and George V are going to be good players. One day we're going to have a team and call it Georgetown.

George Foreman

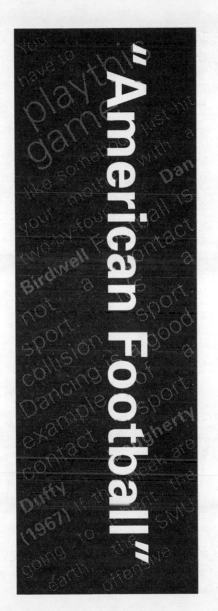

"American Football"

Aggressive Tendencies

You have to play this game like somebody just hit your mother with a two-by-four.

Dan Birdwell

Football is not a contact sport. It's a collision sport. Dancing is a good example of a contact sport.

Duffy Daugherty (1967)

If the meek are going to inherit the earth, the SMU offensive linemen are going to be land barons.

Bill Muir

Animal Instinct

Playing middle linebacker is like walking through a lion's cage dressed in a three-piece pork-chop suit.

Cecil Johnson

If me and King Kong went into an alley, only one of us would come out. And it wouldn't be the monkey.

Lyle Alzado

Dick Butkus was like Moby Dick in a goldfish bowl.

Steve Sabol

Terry Bradshaw couldn't spell cat, if you spotted him the 'C' and the 'A'.

Thomas 'Hollywood' Henderson

When Larry Csonka goes on safari, the lions roll up *their* windows.

Anon

On wide receiver Anthony Carter – I've never seen such skinny legs on a football player before. I wonder if they ever caught the rustler who stole his calves?

Steve Jordan

Rugby is a beastly game played by gentlemen.
Soccer is a gentleman's game played by beasts.
Football is a beastly game played by beasts.

Harry Blaha (1972)

College football is a sport that bears the same relation to education that bullfighting does to agriculture.

Elbert Hubbard

After being pelted with oranges at the Orange Bowl game – I'm glad we're not going to the Gator Bowl.

Lou Holtz (1977)

Bowl Movements

If the Super Bowl is the ultimate game, why are they playing it again next year?

Duane Thomas

More than being concerned with who's going to win the Super Bowl, I feel the Lord is probably more concerned that they find a day other than Sunday to play it on.

Billy Graham

If I'm not selected for the Pro Bowl this year, Stevie Wonder must be counting the ballots.

Otis Wilson (1985)

The Rose Bowl is the only bowl I've ever seen that I didn't have to clean.

Erma Brombeck

Coaching Ins And Outs

A football coach is a person who is willing to lay down your life for the good of his team.

Anon

I knew it was time to quit coaching when I was chewing out an official and he walked off the penalty faster than I could keep up with him.

George Halas

A good football coach needs a patient wife, a loyal dog and a great quarterback – but not necessarily in that order.

Bud Grant

If you're a pro coach, NFL stands for 'Not For Long'.

Jerry Glanville

If a nuclear bomb is ever dropped on the United States, the only things that will survive are Astroturf and coach Don Shula.

Charles 'Bubba' Smith

Coach Jim Walden has the Midas touch – everything he touches turns to mufflers.

Steve Raible

Coach Woody Hayes doesn't know anything about drugs – he thinks uppers are dentures.

Archie Griffin

On why he sacked his head coach – I gave George Allen an unlimited budget and he exceeded it.

Edward B. Williams

English View

The game of football is played all over the world. In some countries, such a game may be called a soccer match. In others, a revolution. However, there are several differences between a football game and a revolution. For one thing, a football game usually lasts longer and the participants wear uniforms. Also, there are usually more casualties in a football game. The object of the game is to move a ball past the other team's goal line. This counts as six points. No points are given for lacerations, contusions, or abrasions, but then no points are deducted either. Kicking is very important in football. In fact, some of the more enthusiastic players even kick the football, occasionally.

Alfred Hitchcock

American football makes rugby look like a Tupperware party.

Sue Lawley (1985)

American football is not so much a sport, but a way of strife. It might best be described as rugby league with knobs on, or feinting by numbers.

Doug Ibbotson

A Fridge Too Far

William 'The Fridge' Perry is the best use of fat since the invention of bacon.

Ray Sons *Chicago Sun Times*

How fast does William Perry run? It all depends on what speed you run the projector!

Buddy Ryan (1986)

It's a good thing William Perry didn't need acupuncture. They'd have to use a harpoon.

Buddy Baron

On his University of Cincinnati football team – We don't have any refrigerators. We have a few pot-belly stoves, but they're on the coaching staff.

Dave Curry

Goal To Go

You've got a goal in life. I've got a goal. Now all we need is a football team.
Groucho Marx

On owning the San Diego Chargers and a major hotel chain – I don't know the difference between a three-point field goal and a 3 p.m. check-out time.
Barron Hilton

Illness And Injury

In this game all you need is speed, strength and an ability to recognise pain immediately.
Reggie Williams (1981)

When you get old, everything is hurting. When I get up in the morning, it sounds like I'm making popcorn.
Lawrence Taylor

One of the great disappointments of a football game is that the cheerleaders never seem to get injured.
New York Tribune

What is a medium collateral whatever ligament? It sounds like spaghetti with fish sauce.
Art Donovan

On suggestions she might date 'Broadway' Joe Namath – Who wants to go with a guy who has two bad knees and a quick release?
Connie Francis

John Riggins, like Joe Namath, is a riddle wrapped in a bandage.
Larry Merchant

I resigned as the Broncos head coach because of illness and fatigue. The fans were sick and tired of me.
John Ralston (1978)

Loss Adjusters

After a loss in which his personal stats were good – It doesn't matter when you lose. It's like putting earrings on a pig – It don't make a whole deal of difference.
Ken Stabler

My only feeling about superstition is that it's unlucky to be behind at the end of the game.
Duffy Daugherty

The game isn't over till Milli Vanilli sing.
Banner at a Green Bay Packers game (1990)

Players

The only qualifications for a lineman are to be big and dumb. To be a back you only have to be dumb.
Knute Rockne

Most football players are temperamental. That's 90 per cent temper and 10 per cent mental.
Doug Plank

Physically, Alonzo Spellman is a world beater. Mentally, he's an egg beater.
Matt Elliott

Mark Gastineau has got an IQ of about room temperature.
Dan Hampton

As a college player at Princeton, I always felt like Dolly Parton's shoulder straps. I knew I had a job to do, but felt totally incapable of doing it.
Jimmy Stewart

On former Wolverines player Gerald Ford – We are very proud of him. He's our first offensive lineman to ever become President.
William Perry

I'm not a mean player. I just try to protect myself. And you'll see I don't ever pick on anybody who has a number above 50!
Mike Ditka

For a while you're a veteran, and then you're just old.
Lance Alworth

If you can keep your head when all about you are losing theirs, you're at the wrong end of the football pitch.
Bill Munro

Run To Daylight

It has been my experience that the fastest man on the football field is the quarterback who has just been intercepted.
Barry Switzer

Franco Harris faked me out so bad one time that I got a 15-yard penalty for grabbing my own face mask.
D. D. Lewis

You've heard of people who zig or zag. Well, Elroy ['Crazy Legs'] Hirsch also had a zog and a couple of zugs.
Norm Van Brocklin

The Shoe Must Go On

Place-kickers aren't footballers, they're hired feet.
Alex Karras

The two most important jobs in America are held by foreigners – room service and goal-kicking.
Beano Cook

Bill Bradley kicks them so high and so short you can't run them back. You have to fair catch every one. Us coaches call that the punt of no return.
Ernal Allen

Football kickers are like taxi cabs. You can always go out and hire another one.
Buddy Ryan (1986)

Teams

On Tampa Bay Buccaneers' difficulties in scoring touchdowns – They should put a sign on the ten-yard line saying: THE BUCS STOP HERE.
Jack Harris

"IceHockey"

Conduct Unbecoming

Ice hockey is a form of disorderly conduct in which the score is kept.
Doug Larson

Aggressive is the hockey word for savage.
Chris Lyndon *Boston Globe*

The key to a hockey match is the first punch. When you're left-handed and they're looking for the right, it helps a lot.
Wayne Cashman

Hockey's the only place where a guy can go nowadays and watch two white guys fight.
Frank Deford

Two people fighting is not violence in hockey. It might be in tennis or bowling, but it's not in hockey.
Gerry Cheevers

He who lives by the cheap shot dies by the crosscheck.
Stan Fischler *Sporting News*

If they took away our sticks and gave us brooms, we'd still have fights.
Phil Esposito (1978)

A puck is a hard rubber disk that hockey players strike when they can't hit each other.
Jimmy Cannon

I went to a fight the other evening and an ice hockey game broke out.
Rodney Dangerfield

Fan To See Hockey

On poor attendances at the LA Kings' home games – There are 800,000 Canadians living in the Los Angeles area, and I've discovered why they left Canada. They hate ice hockey.

Jack Kent Cooke

Hockey is where a fan pays his money and, almost a fifth of the time, sees nothing decided.

Robert Fachet *New York Herald Tribune* **(1978)**

Mental Alert

On not wearing a helmet – The guys tell me I have nothing to protect. No brain, no pain.

Randy Carlyle

This game is 50 per cent mental and 50 per cent being mental.

Jim McKenny

If you take the game seriously, you go crazy anyway, so it helps if you're a bit nuts to start with because you don't waste time getting that way.

Bob Plager

Basketball is the one sport that can be truly influenced by one man. Baseball and football can't, and hockey no one understands anyway.

Pat Williams

Money Grabbing

The three important elements of hockey are: forecheck, backcheck and paycheck.

Gil Perreault

My former wife made me a millionaire. I used to have three million dollars.

Bobby Hull

The National Hockey League is so tightly organised that even the robber barons of old couldn't have devised a more monopolistic feudal system.

Nick Auf der Maur *Last Post* **(1971)**

Performance Heart

To his faltering US Olympic team – Every day you guys look worse and worse. And today you played like tomorrow.

John Mariucci

If you've only got one day to live, come see the Toronto Maple Leafs. It'll seem like forever.

Pat Foley

On his lacklustre Vancouver Canucks – Last season we couldn't win at home and we were losing on the road. My failure was that I couldn't think of any place else to play.

Harry Neale

On his dream – To get as many goals this year as Wayne Gretzky got last week.

Don Maloney

After sacking the stadium organist – Playing *Send In The Clowns* when the referee and the officials went on to the ice was inappropriate, and was compounded when he played *Three Blind Mice* when they left.
Anon Nottingham Panthers official

Players

American professional athletes are bilingual: they speak English and profanity.
Gordie Howe (1975)

On Reebok's new inflatable footwear – Back home the only thing we had with a pump was the well.
Dave Tippett

Goaltending is a normal job, sure. How would you like it in your job if every time you made a small mistake, a red light went on over your desk and 15,000 people stood up and yelled at you?
Jacques Plante

Some nights, Rob Blake looks like Bobby Orr out there. Other nights, however, he looks like iron ore.
Tom Webster

Wet And Wild

After playing in Madison Square Garden – I've seen better ice on the roads in Saskatchewan.
Emile Francis

"Other Sports"

WINNING MAY NOT BE EVERYTHING, BUT IT SURE AS HELL BEATS THE DOG SH*T OUT OF WHAT COMES SECOND.

Anon American saying

Angling

The commonly-accepted source of the term 'angling' is an ancient Indo-European word *anka*, meaning 'hook' or 'to fish with hook', but several other words are also likely candidates, including *enka* (unwise expenditure or useless task), *unglo* (one who is tormented by insects), *onku* (loud or infrequent lamentation), *angi* (to deceive), *onklo* (possession by demons), and *angla* (love of pointless suffering).

Henry Beard *An Angler's Dictionary* (1983)

I would rather go home empty-handed after a day playing a dry fly than catch monsters with a deep-sunk lure dressed like a saloon-bar slut.

Max Hastings *Independent* (1989)

Very little is known of the Canadian country since it's rarely visited by anyone but the Queen and illiterate sports fishermen.

P. J. O'Rourke *National Lampoon* (1976)

A fisherman is a sportsman who catches fish sometimes by patience, sometimes by luck, but most often by the tale.

Leo Baker

An angler is a man who spends his rainy days sitting around on the muddy banks of rivers doing nothing because his wife won't let him do it at home.

The Irish News

Some African natives fish in a prone position. In this country most anglers lie standing up with their arms outstretched.

London Opinion

The formal term for a collection of fishermen is an exaggeration of anglers.

Henry Beard An Angler's Dictionary (1983)

Fishermen and hypochondriacs have one thing in common – they don't have to catch anything to be happy.

Robert Orben

Here's a truth men can perceive
As wholly everlasting:
Oh, what a tangled web they weave
When first they practise fly casting.

Annis Poland

It has always been my private conviction that any man who pits his intelligence against a fish and loses has it coming.

John Steinbeck

I won't die at a match, I might die being dragged down the River Trent by a giant salmon, but at a football match, no.

Jack Charlton (1988)

Someone just back of you while you are fishing is as bad as someone looking over your shoulder while you write a letter to your girl.

Ernest Hemingway

There are two types of fisherman – those who fish for sport and those who fish for fish.

Anon

Given the enormous number of different fishing techniques, very few maxims have universal application, but the handful that are, are worth committing to memory:
a. Never drink beer in waders.
b. Never fish with a vicar.
c. Don't tell jokes in canoes.
d. On ocean-going boats, always fish to the windward.
e. On camping trips, always bring books with large, soft pages.
f. Don't take advice from people with missing fingers.

Henry Beard An Angler's Dictionary (1983)

A thoughtful wife is one who has a juicy steak ready when her husband returns from a day's fishing.

Anon

Fishing is the sport of drowning worms.

Anon

A trout is a fish mainly known by hearsay. It lives on anything not included in a fisherman's equipment.

H. I. Philips

Wahoo: 1. Salt-water game-fish in the mackerel family. 2. Remark made by an angler who inadvertently sits on a treble-hooked salt-water fishing lure.
Henry Beard *An Angler's Dictionary* (1983)

Archery

Poetry is an absolutely dead art – like taking up archery.
Sacheverell Sitwell (1976)

Arm Wrestling

You get guys taking part from M.I.T. [Massachusetts Institute of Technology] and guys who can't spell M.I.T.
Sylvester Stallone

Australian Rules Football

That's not football, mate, it's aerial ping-pong.
Frank Hardy *The Yarns of Billy Borker* (1965)

Without giving offence to anyone, I may remark that it is a game which commends itself to semi-barbarous races.
Edward Kinglake *The Australian at Home* (1891)

Australian Rules football might best be described as a game devised for padded cells, played in the open air.
James Murray

Bobsleigh and Luge

What I'm trying to get over to the public is that bobsleighing isn't solely populated by people from the gossip columns looking for a little exercise after another night in Annabel's.
Prince Michael of Kent (1980)

Bobsledding is a sport in which demented people sit on a sled that goes 2,000 miles per hour down an ice ditch. The same sport is often practised without ice – when four drunks leave a fraternity party in a BMW.
Dan Jenkins *Playboy* (1988)

On his role as brakeman – You start out as Raging Bull and then turn into Tinkerbell.
Herschel Walker (1992)

After trying out the luge run at Calgary – It was what I would call the ultimate laxative.
Otto Jelinek

Body Building

If nature had intended our skeletons to be visible it would have put them on the outside of our bodies.
Elmer Rice

Body builders do not throw their weight around – they flaunt it.
David Hunn

The whole point of this so-called body building, I gather, is to get rid of the attractive flesh on the surface and to display all the working bits underneath.

Kenneth Robinson

On oiling their skin for a competition – These body builders have got to be careful. If you use too much you look like a glazed doughnut.

Bob Birdsong (1973)

It does not befit a man to parade in front of the public flexing his muscles. They don't walk, they carry their muscled torsos proudly – self-conceited, self-important, looking like roosters on a promenade. There are very many unbalanced persons among them. Men who take anabolic steroids and men in their thirties who don't want to get married.

Sovetsky Sport **(1978)**

Bowling (Lawn)

On Crown Green bowlers playing lawn bowls – It's like a street-fighter conforming to the Marquis of Queensberry rules.

Tony Allcock

Bowls are built with a bias, and so for that matter are many of the players.

Herbert Collings

Bowling (Ten-Pin)

One of the advantages bowling has over golf is that you seldom lose a bowling ball.
Don Carter

Labour's and management dislikes
Dismay me more and more;
The only place I'm free from strikes
Is in my bowling score.
Avery Giles

Bullfighting

A bull is heavy, violent, abusive, and aggressive, with four legs and great sharp teeth – whereas a bullfighter is only a small greasy Spaniard.
Monty Python's Flying Circus

At a bullfight in sunny Madrid,
A tourist went right off his lid.
He made straight for the bull,
While the crowd yelled, "The fool
Will go home on a slab!" And he did!
Anon

Chess

Chess is a game that is played on squares by squares. **Anon**

Chess is as elaborate a waste of human intelligence as you can find outside an advertising agency.
Raymond Chandler

I failed to make the chess team, because of my height.
Woody Allen

Chess can be described as the movement of pieces eating one another.
Marcel Duchamp *Art News* (1969)

It is impossible to win gracefully at chess. No man has yet said 'Mate!' in a voice which failed to sound to his opponent bitter, boastful and malicious.
A. A. Milne *Not That It Matters* (1919)

On being asked if he was friendly with Anatoly Karpov – Do the Yankees like the Red Sox?
Gary Kasparov

On the Kasparov–Short World Championship – Whatever gave Channel 4 the idea that two ugly blokes moving chess pieces would make interesting TV?
New Musical Express (1994)

Commentating on Manchester United v Leeds United – It may be interesting but the game has all the excitement of Channel 4's coverage of the World Chess Championships.
Ron Jones, BBC Radio 5 (1994)

Climbing

The only thing on the level is mountain climbing.
Eddie Quinn

Mount Everest is very easy to climb, only just a little too high.
André Roche

After climbing Mount McKinley – The view from the top is not worth the climb.
Bernard Segger

Croquet

Croquet is no game for the soft of sinew and the gentle of spirit. The higher and dirtier croquet can use the guile of a cobra and the inhumanity of a boa constrictor. Then, the general physique of a stevedore comes in handy, too.

Alexander Woollcott

Croquet is like an embalming fluid. It keeps you in the same state for ever. Only trouble is, most people don't begin to play until they're getting on, so it's not exactly a preservative of youth.
Anon (1978)

To peg out, or not to peg out – that is the question.
John W. Solomon (1966)

Croquet is to be distinguished from cricket and chicken croquettes, which is a culinary term. It is ten times more exciting than tiddlywinks.
Nigel Aspinall (1973)

The clunk of the ball against mallet is a lovely sound, just like ice cubes in a gin and tonic.
The Sunday Times (1987)

Something like 50,000 US-made croquet sets are sold per year, and with them 50,000 conflicting sets of rules.
New York Times (1978)

Hurlingham rules, Croquet.
Graffiti

Cycling

The first cycle race probably took place as soon as the second bicycle was completed.

J. Else *The A–Z of Cycling* **(1978)**

On receiving the MBE – It rates just above being given a Blue Peter badge.

Chris Boardman (1993)

Darts

I was watching Sumo wrestling on the television for two hours before I realised it was darts.

Hattie Hayridge (1989)

I had a bash at positive thinking, yoga, transcendental meditation, even hypnosis. They only screwed me up, so now I'm back to my normal game – a couple of lagers.

Leighton Rees (1984)

It was an easy decision to turn pro – I was unemployed.

Jocky Wilson (1990)

I've been described as fat, boozy and toothless. That's pretty accurate.

Jocky Wilson (1982)

Jocky Wilson is the minimum of mass into which a human being can be contracted.

Nancy Banks-Smith *The Guardian* **(1990)**

John Lowe's so boring. All he talks about is his home and his car. Still, for a welder, he's done well.

Eric Bristow (1989)

If Eric Bristow was at Cape Canaveral, he'd take off before the rocket.

Sid Waddell

Tony Brown attacks his opponents the same way Desperate Dan attacks cow pie.

Sid Waddell

Dennis Priestley's darts are going in to the 60 at more angles than Hypotenuse ever dreamed of.

Sid Waddell, Sky Sports TV (1996)

On the similar-looking Phil Taylor and Dennis Priestley, in the 1996 World Darts Championship Final – Luckily they differed in the costume department. Phil wore a blue shirt with bits of tin foil stuck to it. Dennis the uniform of his cartoon-character nickname: Bozo v Beano.

Andrew Baker *Independent on Sunday* **(1996)**

Greyhound Racing

No dog can go as fast as the money you bet on him.

'Bud' Flanagan

My grandfather couldn't prescribe a pill to make a greyhound run faster, but he could produce one to make the other five go slower.

Benny Green (1972)

Gymnastics

A gymnast is one who wears spring and fall clothing at the same time.
Anon

The general idea is to keep mass to a minimum, so that girls can achieve speed without momentum. Breasts look exactly like shoulder blades. Nelli Kim, who won a stack of gold medals, is almost an anachronism, being in possession of a detectable bottom.
Clive James (1981)

In Russia, show the least athletic aptitude and they've got you dangling off the parallel bars with a leotard full of hormones.
Victoria Wood *Up to you Porky* **(1985)**

Hang-Gliding

If at first you don't succeed, so much for hang-gliding.
Anon

Hang-gliding is just a breeze.
Anon

Hang-gliding is done on a wing and a prayer.
Anon

Hang-gliding, blast baseball, and sod cycling.
Anon

Gliding is a team sport, up to the point at which you become airborne.
Bill Scull, national gliding coach

Hockey

After a rain-soaked win against Olympic champions Spain – It was worth getting your knickers wet for.
Jenny Cardwell (1992)

Ice Skating

Ice skating – with its meticulously preordinated choreography, fanciful dress and movements that consist of wandering around in apparently pointless, ever-decreasing circles – is closer to Trooping the Colour than to a sport
Julie Burchill *Only a Game*

Olympic figure skating – a sport where competitors are dressed as dinner mints.
Jere Longman *Philadelphia Inquirer*

This is a sport where you talk about sequins, earrings and plunging necklines – and you are talking about the men.
Christine Brennan *Washington Post*

Skating is elegant, it's safe, and it's indoors. You can see some great legs on the girls and a lot of guys who'd make damn fine waiters.
Dan Jenkins *Playboy* **(1988)**

On his partnership with Jayne Torvill – We are so tied together that we are almost a brand name.
Christopher Dean (1993)

Jayne Torvill looks like a London housewife attending the wedding of one of her children.
Jean-Christophe Papillon (1994)

It has always seemed to me hard luck on the very best ice-dancing skaters that they have to spend so much of their time whizzing along backwards, with their bottoms sticking rather undecoratively out.
Arthur Marshall *Sunday Telegraph* **(1986)**

During the 1980 Winter Olympics – Jan Hoffmann knocked off the triples with the awesome precision of a fighter pilot swatting flies. He made the same artistic impression as a fringe theatre company producing a minor play by Brecht in the back room of a pub.
Clive James

On meeting the heavily bejewelled Liberace – You've got so much ice on your hands I could skate on them.
John Curry (1977)

If I can't defrost this refrigerator pretty soon, I can rent it to Peggy Fleming to rehearse in.
Cher (1975)

Take speed skating ... people wearing leotards and shower caps, swinging one arm, skate round the oval until *Sports Illustrated* stops taking pictures.
Dan Jenkins *Playboy* **(1988)**

Pairs skating is doing it in public without scaring the horses.
Alan Coren

Lacrosse

They thought lacrosse was what you find in la church.
Robin Williams *Playboy* **(1982)**

Netball

Netball is an outlet – an escape from the humdrum. There's nothing gives me such a kick. Well, nothing except vodka.
Angela Farley (1989)

Powerboating

Driving a powerboat is a bit like having one person throw a bucket of water over you while another hits you with a baseball bat.
Steve Curtis (1989)

I know nothing of engines. There could be five rabbits in there for all I know.
Betty Cook (1977)

Rifle Shooting

Contrary to popular belief, we do not put the two teams at opposite ends of the range.
Tom Jones

Roller Skating

The hardest thing about roller skating is the ground.

Anon

I have recently taken up two new sports: roller skating and ankle spraining, in that order. I am getting quite good at both.

Miles Kington *The Perils of Roller Skating*

Rowing

Show me a crazy rower who has fallen out of a one-man boating race, and I'll show you a man who is out of his scull.

Anon

Henley Regatta is full of haughty happiness, hats, haves and very few have-nots.

Frank Keating *The Guardian* (1983)

Henley was so wet this year it should have been renamed Duckley.

Jilly Cooper *Turn Right at the Spotted Dog*

You talk about the Rose Bowl, you can have your World Series or Heavyweight Championship, but when a US oarsman, any oarsman, hears the crowd cheer at Henley he's heard everything. Anybody at Henley knows what he's talking about. They can tell you how to start, how to row the middle, when to spurt – and what the hell's wrong with your number five man.

Randy Jablonic (1970)

The Oxford–Cambridge Boat Race would be much more attractive if the rules were changed to allow the boats to ram each other.

Miles Kington

After the Boat Race course had been explained to him – Don't you think it's going to be rather wet for the horses?

Spike Milligan

After a dead heat in the Boat Race – Oxford won, Cambridge too!

***Punch* (1877)**

On Sue Brown, the first female cox in the University Boat Race – The only occupant of the Oxford boat smaller than a house was the coxette. Weighing about as much as the stroke's left thigh.

Clive James (1981)

Ah! Isn't that nice, the wife of the Cambridge president is kissing the cox of the Oxford crew.

Harry Carpenter, BBC TV (1977)

Skiing

Skiing is the only sport where you can spend an arm and a leg to break an arm and a leg.

Henry Beard *Skiing* (1989)

Skiing? Why break my leg at 40 degrees below zero when I can fall downstairs at home?

Corey Ford

There are really only three things to learn in skiing: how to put on your skis, how to slide downhill, and how to walk along the hospital corridor.
Lord Mancroft *A Chinaman in the Bath* **(1974)**

St Moritz, the heart of the broken-limb country, where a man must prove himself first on skis and then on a stretcher.
Art Buchwald *I Chose Caviar* **(1957)**

In St Moritz everyone who is anything goes around in plaster, which may be fashionable, but is damned uncomfortable. I value my legs as much as Marlene Dietrich values hers.
Noel Coward

I do not participate in any sport with ambulances at the bottom of the hill.
Erma Brombeck

I used to be with three women until 5 a.m. Now I'm in training, it's five women until 3 a.m.
Alberto Tomba (1992)

There are two main forms of this sport: Alpine skiing and Nordic skiing. Alpine involves a mountain and a $5,000 to $10,000 investment, plus $300,000 for the condo in Aspen and however much you spend on drugs. It is a sport only a handful of people ever master, and those who do, do so at the expense of other skills like talking and writing their own name.
National Lampoon **(1979)**

The sport of skiing consists of wearing 3,000 dollars' worth of clothes and equipment, and driving 2,000 miles in the snow in order to stand around at a bar and get drunk.
P. J. O'Rourke *Modern Manners* **(1983)**

Skis are a pair of long, thin, flexible runners that permit a skier to slide across the snow and into debt.
Henry Beard *Skiing* **(1989)**

A ski jacket is the larval stage of a blimp.
Henry Beard *Skiing* **(1989)**

On winning the World downhill crown – I just did my best, and for once, it was good enough.
Hansjorge Tauscher (1989)

I went skiing and I knew I was going too fast when I suddenly realised that I was actually getting younger.
John Ross

On taking part in the Olympic downhill – We have no word for downhill in Senegalese because we have no mountains. I was so afraid I almost threw up. I have fully tested the safety measures and I can tell you they work.
Lamine Gueye

We skiers know that falling over isn't important; it's getting up again.
Gerald Ford

Coaching women isn't much different from coaching men – just as long as you remember they are women.
Hank Tauber (1970)

If God had meant Texans to ski, He would have made bullsh*t white.

Anon

The word slalom means 'slope tracks' and it comes from Norway, like many other commonly used skiing terms including 'oops' (a fall), 'blammo' (a collision with a tree), 'floo' (a bad cold), 'glopp' (food served at a mountain lunch stop), and 'fokkendolt' (a skier who runs into other skiers).

Henry Beard *Skiing* **(1989)**

In the biathlon, a Russian puts on a pair of skis, picks up a rifle, slides around in the trees, and stops every so often to shoot a West German.

Dan Jenkins *Playboy* **(1988)**

Ski Jumping

A skier is a person who jumps to contusions.

Anon

All the demented people who aren't bobsledders are ski jumpers. The athlete comes down the world's tallest playground slide ... hoping to land somewhere near a quaint little village below.

Dan Jenkins *Playboy* **(1988)**

Matti Nykaenen is a bird. It's like somebody sucked all the marrow from his bones and replaced it with helium.

Matt Peri (1988)

Eddie Edwards doesn't fly – he just drops out the sky. It's not ski jumping.

Rob McCormack (1988)

What about Eddie the bloody stupid Eagle? Don't tell me he's a sportsman ... thick as two short planks.

Eric Bristow (1989)

Eddie's glasses are pink and white and as thick as the bottom of a Coca-Cola bottle, and when he puts his goggles over them they mist up.

Chris Brasher (1988)

Mr Edwards' Olympic performance was the equivalent of a first-ball duck in a Test match, two own goals in a Wembley Cup Final, or a first round 168 in the Open Championship.

Ian Wooldridge *Daily Mail* **(1988)**

We have thousands of Eddie Edwards in Norway, but we never let them jump.

Torbjorn Yggeseth (1988)

Snooker, Billiards and Pool

Billiards is very similar to snooker, except there are only three balls and no one watches it.

Steve Davis (1988)

On sex in the movies – The British Board of Censors will not pass any seduction scene unless the seducer has one foot on the floor. Apparently, sex in England is something like snooker.

Fred Allen

I think it's great to talk during sex, as long as it's about snooker.
Steve Davis

On the imminent birth of his first child – We weren't hoping for a boy or girl, we were just happy to take pot luck.
Steve Davis

Sport is cut and dried. You always know when you succeed. You are not an actor; you don't wonder, 'Did my performance go down well tonight?'. You've lost.
Steve Davis

On the rewards for his first televised maximum break – I refuse to make another 147. Stephen Hendry has just made one in the World Championships and got £147,000. Jimmy White got £100,000 a couple of years ago in the World Championships ... I got a Lada car.
Steve Davis

On his 'boring' style – I suppose the charisma bypass operation was a big disappointment in my life.
Steve Davis

People say that because of a lady's shape, it isn't possible for them to play snooker well. That shape hasn't prevented Bill Werbeniuk earning a decent living.
Allison Fisher (1986)

Playing snooker gives you firm hands and helps to build up character. It is the ideal recreation for dedicated nuns.
Archbishop Luigi Barbarito (1989)

After a heavy defeat – I played like a slow puncture.
John Parrott (1989)

I don't want to be a superstar, I just want superstar money.
James Wattana (1992)

And that's the third time he's missed his waistcoat pocket with the chalk.
Ted Lowe, BBC TV

Jimmy White has a flair for living. When he was 12, he was as worldly as a 40-year-old and as naive as a four-year-old. Jimmy could work out a yankee, but couldn't name the capital of France.
Barry Hearn (1989)

On Dennis Taylor's oversized glasses – You look like Mickey Mouse with a welding shield on.
Eddie Charlton

Stephen Hendry is the only man with a face that comes with free garlic bread.
Nick Hancock *They Think It's All Over* **BBC TV (1995)**

Alex Higgins' autobiography is called *Alex Through the Looking Glass* ... *Through The Plate Glass Window* would have been more appropriate.
Nick Hancock *They Think It's All Over* **BBC TV (1995)**

Back in Belfast, someone threw Alex Higgins a petrol bomb and he drank it.
Frank Carson

A lot of people are using two-piece cues, nowadays. Alex Higgins hasn't got one, because they don't come with instructions.

Steve Davis

Bums play pool, gentlemen play billiards.

Daniel McGoorty

When I realised that what I had turned out to be was a lousy, two-bit pool hustler and drunk, I wasn't depressed at all, I was glad to have a profession.

Daniel McGoorty

Try to hate your opponent. Even if you are playing your grandmother, try to beat her 50 to nothing. If she already has three, try to beat her 50 to three.

Daniel McGoorty

Dressing a pool player in a tuxedo is like putting whipped cream on a hot dog.

Minnesota Fats

Every pool player's an egotist. You get four drinks inside a guy and he's never lost a game; you get ten drinks in him and he's never missed a shot.

Don Willis

Greater love hath no man than to lay down his life behind the eight ball.

Luther Lassiter

Squash

To walk from the squash court to the dressing room as weak as a kitten, sweat dripping off you but mind as clear as tomorrow's dawn, is better than five reefers or a trip on LSD.
John Hopkins (1971)

Squash – that's not exercise, it's flagellation.
Noel Coward

If you think squash is a competitive sport, try flower arrangement.
Alan Bennett *Talking Heads* (1988)

Surfing

A surfer is an American lemming.
Jacob Bronowski

Swimming

Swimming is the only sport in which before an athlete competes, he stands on a pedestal, is introduced and applauded. He hasn't even done anything yet.
Mark Spitz (1976)

I'm a woman first and a swimmer second. I attract trouble like worms attract birds.
Dawn Fraser (1965)

I wanted to be an Olympic swimmer, but I had some problems with buoyancy.
Woody Allen

One of the girls in my squad complained that there were men in the women's changing room at a recent gala in Vienna, only for the chaperone to discover that she had merely overheard East German girls in the next cubicle.
Charles Wilson

On her girls' 'deep' voices – We have come here to swim, not to sing.
Anon East German Olympic swimming coach (1976)

On losing the Olympic 100 metres freestyle final – I'd like to be a superhero all my life, but today my cape fell off.
Matt Biondi (1994)

On not taking steroids – I've got a career that depends a lot on being tall and blonde, and if I ended up growing a beard I don't think it would do me much good.
Sharron Davies (1989)

Spearfishing is an angling method that combines the sports of diving, fishing, and if sharks are sighted, Olympic swimming.
Henry Beard *An Angler's Dictionary* (1983)

What on earth has this synchronised swimming got to do with anything, let alone sport?
Frank Keating *The Guardian* (1984)

What I have never been able to discover is whether the fellows who swim the Channel are obliged to keep their feet off the ground all the way.
E. V. Knox *It Occurs to Me*

Alison Streeter is an amazingly fast swimmer. A 30-second channel crossing puts her speed at some 2,400 mph – no, hang on, poor radio reception, that was her 32nd channel crossing. Still, another world record for Alison, making her more reliable than the Chunnel. On her next crossing, she will tow a Ford Transit filled with 600 bottles of Stella Artois.

Tom Bussman *The Guardian* (1995)

Volleyball

Most people think that volleyball is 22 people on the beach who quit playing when the hamburgers are ready.

Steve Timmons

Water Skiing

The problem with water skiing is the risk of a 30 mph enema.

Anon

Water skiing is the only form of skiing in which skiers can't end up by accident in a place that is too steep for them.

Henry Beard *Skiing* (1989)

Barefoot water skiing is no personal ambition, particularly when the World Championships take place alongside an Essex shopping centre car park.

David Hunn *The Sunday Times* (1992)

Weightlifting

If somebody told weightlifters they could lift an extra five pounds by munching Brillo pads, there wouldn't be a clean pot within three miles of any gym in this country.

Mark Cameron

Sure I was once a 97-pound weakling. When I was four years old.

Paul Anderson

After four of seven Canadian Olympic weightlifters had been banned for drug abuse – Canadian weightlifters: three clean and four jerks.

Olympic Village graffiti

Wrestling

Professional wrestling's most mysterious hold is on its audience.

Luke Neely (1953)

Wrestlers often trade punches that wouldn't knock the dust off an heirloom and apply holds that a girl scout could break.

Wrestling Review **(1966)**

I believe that professional wrestling is clean and everything else in the world is fixed.

Frank Deford

If it's all-in, why do they wrestle?

Mae West

When asked how he pronounced his name – Just the way it is spelled.

Meriyam Tsalkalamanidze

During the 1994 football World Cup – Of course, Americans prefer their sport predictable and uniform. And you begin to understand why they lap up things like the World Wrestling Federation.

Martin Smith *Daily Telegraph* **(1994)**

Professional wrestling is the only sport where participants are just thrown right out into the audience, and no one in the crowd thinks anything is happening. If you're watching a golf tournament and Jack Nicklaus goes flying over your head – first of all, I would say, you're watching a very competitive tournament.

Jerry Seinfeld *Seinlanguage* **(1993)**

I don't know what it is, but I can't look at Hulk Hogan and believe that he's the end result of millions and millions of years of evolution.

Jim Murray

Hello! magazine is to serious issues what the *WWF Sticker Album* is to children's literature.

Mary Riddell *Daily Mirror* **(1992)**

Yachting

Yacht racing: A popular nautical contact sport.

Henry Beard *A Sailor's Dictionary* **(1981)**

The things that drive a man to ocean sailing must be pretty much the same as those that drive him to drink.

Hugh Whall (1966)

Watching an America's Cup is like watching the grass grow.

Ring Lardner

After an Australian yacht sank in the America's Cup trials –

Q. What's the difference between a tea bag and oneAustralia?

A. A tea bag stays in the Cup longer.

After the San Diego Yacht Club won the America's Cup – All those kids raised in the slums of Beverly Hills and Newport Beach now see sailing as their way out of the ghetto.

Jay Leno

I am not interested in sailing around the world. Not that there is any lack of requests for me to do so.

Edward Heath (1977)

Ocean racing is like standing under a cold shower tearing up £5 notes.

Edward Heath

There is never a right time to sail across the Atlantic alone. There is only a now or never.

David Blagden (1973)

A coarse sailor is one who, in a crisis, forgets nautical language and shouts, 'For God's sake, turn left!'.

Michael Green *The Art of Coarse Sailing* **(1962)**

Coarse sailing is not mucking about in boats but boating about in muck.

Michael Green *The Art of Coarse Sailing* **(1962)**

"General"

I am getting to an age when I can only enjoy the last sport left. It is called hunting for your spectacles.
Lord Grey (1927)

War is the only game in which it doesn't pay to have home-court advantage.
Dick Motta

Sport is the only entertainment where, no matter how many times you go back, you never know the ending.
Neil Simon

Amateur

The only real sporting amateur is one who pays his own expenses.
Vivian Jenkins

Amateur: one who plays games for the love of the thing. Unlike the professional, he receives no salary, and is contented with presents of clothes, clubs, rackets, cigarettes, cups, cheques, hotel expenses, fares, and so on.
J. B. Morton (Beachcomber) *Daily Express*

Anti-Sport

When it comes to sports, I am not particularly interested. Generally speaking, I look upon them as dangerous and tiring activities performed by people with whom I share nothing except the right to trial by jury.
Fran Lebowitz *Metropolitan Life* (1978)

Astroturf

If horses can't eat it, I won't play on it.
Dick Allen

Balls

Spring is the season of balls – golf, tennis, base and moth.
L. L. Levinson

Disabled

On the lack of funding for disabled sports – Ready, willing and disabled.
Kevin Mitchell *The Observer* (1994)

On being asked if her wheelchair made it more difficult to loose off her archery bow – I don't know. I've never shot standing up.
Neroli Fairhill

On the Toronto Blue Jays' rowdy fans – Most of them would heckle the Special Olympics.
Dennis Lamp

Exercise

Contrary to popular, cable-TV-induced opinion, aerobics have absolutely nothing to do with squeezing our body into hideous shiny Spandex, grinning like a deranged orang-utan, and doing cretinous dance steps to debauched disco music.
Cynthia Heimel *Sex Tips for Girls* (1983)

My idea of exercise is a good brisk sit.
Phyllis Diller

I bought all those Jane Fonda videos. I love to sit and eat cookies and watch 'em.
Dolly Parton

As a nation we are dedicated to keeping physically fit – and parking as close to the stadium as possible.
Bill Vaughan

If God had meant me to exercise, He'd put diamonds on the floor.
Joan Rivers

Walking may be good exercise, but did you ever see a postman as well built as a truck driver?
Anon

Skipping is the best exercise to lose weight – skipping lunch, skipping dinner.
Anon

I used to think squat thrusts were a gym test until I discovered Greek toilets.
Graffiti

The need for exercise is a modern superstition, invented by people who ate too much, and had nothing to think about.
George Santayana

Jogging

Show me a man who jogs every morning and I'll show you a breaking marriage.
Kenneth Robinson

It's unnatural for people to run around the city streets unless they are thieves or victims. It makes people nervous to see someone running. I know that when I see someone running on my street, my instincts tell me to let the dog go after him.

Mike Royko

Jogging is for people who aren't intelligent enough to watch breakfast television.

Victoria Wood (1989)

Exactly how intricate a sport is jogging? You were two years old. You ran after the cat. You pretty much had it mastered.

Rick Reilly *Sports Illustrated* **(1992)**

Joggers are basically neurotic, bony, smug types who could bore the paint off a DC-10. It is a scientifically proven fact that having to sit through a three-minute conversation between two joggers will cause your IQ to drop 13 points.

Rick Reilly, *Ibid*

My doctor told me jogging could add years to my life. I told him, 'Yeah, since I began, I already feel ten years older!'

Lee Trevino

If God had meant us to run on pavements, He'd have given us radial toes.

Dennis Norden

Joggers aren't very friendly. They pant rather than speak. If you get in their way, they run over you rather than stop in their stride, or they stand impatiently, moving their legs up and down and shaking their hands. Joggers don't have time to talk to each other. Joggers can't help you get the rock out of your shoe. Joggers are intent on finishing.

Emily Herring Wilson

The only reason I would take up jogging is so that I could hear heavy breathing again.

Erma Brombeck

The only thing running and exercise can do for you is to make you healthy.

Mickey Lolich

I don't jog. If I die I want to be sick.

Abe Lemmons

Running requires no special skills. It is often more beneficial to jog around the psychiatrist's building than to enter – and cheaper than the couch.

Anon

Money

Perhaps sport should accept sponsorship from the Mafia. They kill fewer people than smoking.

Alan Hubbard *The Observer* **(1994)**

Money has done more than make the sports world go round, it has made it spin off its axis.

Gary Pomerantz

Never bet on a dead horse or a live woman. Never play cards with a man with dark glasses or his own deck.

Jim Murray

Officials

I wanted to have a career in sports when I was young, but I had to give it up. I'm only six feet tall, so I couldn't play basketball. I'm only 190 pounds, so I couldn't play football. And I have 20–20 vision, so I couldn't be a referee.

Jay Leno (1993)

Olympics

Murphy's Law and Parkinson's Law have both contributed to an Olympics Law which says that the bigger a thing becomes, the more problems it attracts and the sooner it hastens its own demise.

Norman Harris *The Observer* (1984)

We may not be the greatest nation at winning Winter Olympics, but at least we can carry our bloody flag properly.

Squadron Leader Mike Freeman, Great Britain bobsleigh team (1972)

People from Los Angeles have come to me for advice now that they've gotten the Games for 1984. I've told them my first piece of advice is 'Give 'em back!'

Reverend Bernard Fell, Lake Placid Olympic Committee (1981)

On Atlanta's Olympic mascot – A little mutant monstrosity that was born in the toxic dump of somebody's imagination.

Los Angeles Times **(1992)**

The Olympics. Not a sport but several peculiar sports … each of which only commands your attention every four years, like a dental appointment.

Dan Jenkins *What Are They?*

Politics

On Denis Howell, Minister for Sport – He is not unlike a 50-pence piece: double-faced, many-sided and intrinsically not worth a great deal.

Wilf Wooller

Exchange in the House of Commons after a debate on soccer ID cards –
Colin Moynihan (Sports Minister): Why did you call me a twister?
Denis Howell (Shadow Sports Minister): Because I couldn't call you a little sh*t.

On athletes in politics – The affluent society tends to pay more attention to what is visually pleasing, hence the emphasis nowadays on Style. It is more fun to elect popular heroes than to make heroes out of businessmen and lawyers. And besides, trained athletes are cool under stress, and know how to drive down the middle of the road, and avoid falling off bridges.

William F. Buckley Jr. *Jock* (1969)

Promoters and Agents

A sports promoter is just a guy with two pieces of bread looking for a piece of cheese.
Evel Knievel

If God had an agent, the world wouldn't be built yet. It'd only be Thursday.
Jerry Reynolds

After calling all sports agents vultures –
It was a rash statement and I'd like to apologise to every vulture in the sky.
Mike Gottfried

Win, Lose Or Draw

What does the result matter – as long as you win.
Ronnie Dawson

In top-class sport, you're the rooster one day, just a feather duster the next.
Alan Jones (1984)

If a tie is like kissing your sister, losing is like kissing your grandmother with her teeth out.
George Brett

Everybody says a tie is like kissing your sister. I guess it's better than kissing your brother.
Lou Holtz

Women

The Ancient Greeks kept women athletes out of their games. They wouldn't even let them on the sidelines. I'm not sure but that they were right.
Avery Brundage (1972)

Women in sport? Who wants straight-legged, narrow-hipped, big-shouldered, powerful sheilas, aggressive and ferocious in mind and body?
Percy Cerrutty (1970)

No man is fit to be called a sportsman what doesn't kick his wife out of bed on an average once in three weeks.
Robert S. Surtees

Since the age of 14, I have dearly wanted to be regarded as a sex object. I am absolutely sick of being loved for my cooking, accurate seam bowling, ability to solve anagrams, and obtain credit from bookmakers, and yet there are women who profess to be fearful of the alternative.
Jeffrey Bernard (1975)

"Sports Media"

STAY TUNED FOR TODAY'S SPRING TRAINING OPENER AGAINST THE CALIFORNIA ANGELS. THIS HAS BEEN THE SAN DIEGO PADRES' POST-GAME SHOW.
Jerry Coleman

The Press Gang

It has often occurred to me that sport, like sex, is an activity that should either be performed or watched – but not written about.
Paul Gardner

The first thing I do every morning is read the sports pages. I read it before I do the front pages because at least on the sports pages you have a 50–50 chance of being right.
Gerald Ford

Sportswriters on television have become as common as rats in a drain. Sportswriters should be read and not seen.
Norman Chad *Sports Illustrated* **(1992)**

Sportswriters have become the insurance salesmen of the 1990s. You don't ever want to get stuck in an elevator with one.
Norman Chad *Ibid*

I once thought of becoming a political cartoonist because they only have to come up with one idea a day. Then I thought I'd become a sportswriter instead, because they don't have to come up with any.
Sam Snead

The capacity of sporting journalists to wax lyrical in the face of the exceptional is only matched by the speed with which they run out of adjectives in doing so.

Derek Malcolm

What's the difference between a three-week-old puppy and a sportswriter? In six weeks, the puppy stops whining.

Mike Ditka

The best three years of a sportswriter's life are the third grade.

George Raveling

How did I get hooked on drugs? Well, it's something like a sportswriter having a drink after work.

Tyrrell Biggs (1988)

The perfect Christmas gift for sportscasters, as all fans of sports clichés know, is a scoreless tie.

William Safire

Philadelphia is the only city in the world where you can experience the thrill of victory and the agony of reading about it the next day.

Mike Schmidt

Sure I know where the press room is – I just look for where they throw the dog meat.

Martina Navratilova (1983)

I've always said there's a place for the press but they haven't dug it yet.

Tommy Docherty (1980)

San Francisco sportswriters describe the baseball scene with all the precision of three-year-old children finger painting on the playroom wall.

Jim Brosnan *The Long Season*

New York sportswriters are busy getting ready for the baseball season. They're going through their thesauruses looking for synonyms for 'dictatorial', 'obnoxious' and 'eliminated'.

David Letterman

After winning the British Open – I would like to thank the press from the heart of my bottom.

Nick Faldo (1992)

On constant media attention – When seagulls follow a trawler, it is because they think sardines will be thrown into the sea.

Eric Cantona (1995)

(*N.B. Cantona's former Leeds United colleague Gordon Strachan spoke for many: If a Frenchman goes on about seagulls, trawlers and sardines, he's called a philosopher. I'd just be called a short Scottish bum talking crap.*)

After covering the America's Cup – The only difference between yachting writers and baseball writers is that yachting writers wear sneakers.

'Red' Smith

I became a sportswriter because, back in my days at *Time* magazine, I was the only one in the building who could spell Carl Yastrzemski.

Jim Murray *Los Angeles Times*

On becoming a baseball columnist – I guess I'll have to gain 60 pounds, start smoking cigars, and wear clothes that don't match.

Gareth Iorg

On The Box

FANTASY FOOTBALL LEAGUE *(BBC TV)*
Transferring this crap to television isn't much of a gamble for BBC 2 as it can only have cost a couple of quid to make.

Ben Olins *The Guardian* **(1993)**

AN EVENING WITH GARY LINEKER *(ITV)*
It might have worked in the theatre, but on TV it looked as misplaced as a subtle, 30-yard chip from Tony Adams ... These boys didn't do great at all.

Charlie Catchpole *News of the World* **(1994)**

GLADIATORS *(ITV)*
The novelty of watching people named after pet Rottweilers hit each other over the head with giant cotton buds was always going to wear off.

Charlie Catchpole *News of the World* **(1992)**

GLADIATORS *(ITV)*
Where presenters [John Fashanu and Ulrika Jonsson] read 'enthusiasm' off an autocue, and the commentator [John Sachs] sounds like a machine.

Margaret Forwood *Daily Express* **(1992)**

MATCH OF THE DAY *(BBC TV)*
The BBC are just *so* straight, *so* respectable, they really can't do without the "Housewives' Choice" sort of people, people like Bobby Charlton and Trevor Brooking. They just will not rock the boat.

Mike Ticher *When Saturday Comes*

A QUESTION OF SPORT *(BBC TV)*
Soviet footballers have an odd penchant for getting killed in car accidents ... Perhaps this is some kind of Slavonic death-wish, the equivalent of appearing regularly on *A Question of Sport*.

Andy Lyons *When Saturday Comes* **(1986)**

RUGBY SPECIAL *(BBC TV)*
Ten of the easiest jobs in the world:
No. 4: Make-up artists on *Rugby Special*.

Journolists *Mail on Sunday*

SAINT AND GREAVSIE *(ITV)*
T is for Television, and the almost surreal brainlessness of *Saint and Greavsie*, with their rehearsed 'conversations', which look about as natural as Peter Reid's black rinse.

Andy Lyons *When Saturday Comes* **(1987)**

TEST MATCH CRICKET *(BBC TV)*
When television voices, at the Test, do surface, it is their timbre rather than idiom which grips – a speech therapist's dream: Ray Illingworth's 'It's not a pulling wicket, this isn't'; the twanging 'eows' and 'ois' that punctuate Denis Compton's carefully refined accent; and Jim Laker's pronunciation is as canny as his old tweakers – if he can say

swinging, why does he say innins and why doesn't he say swinnin?
Martin Amis *New Statesman* **(1975)**

THERE'S ONLY ONE BRIAN MOORE *(ITV)* – The usually funny Bob Mills takes football far too seriously, like so many men in cheap suits and hair gel who pontificate about 'the great game' in beer-swilling bonding sessions.
Josephine Monroe *Time Out* **(1995)**

His Master's Voice

There are two professions that one can be hired at with little experience. One is prostitution. The other is sportscasting. Too frequently, they become the same.
Howard Cosell

A colour commentator is a guy who's paid to talk while everyone goes to the bathroom.
Bill Curry (1968)

Sports announcers are as colourless as a glass of gin.
Bill Curry

We're beginning to understand the sportscaster. For example, when one of his favourite teams loses – that's an upset.
Edward Stevenson

To get a job you've either got to be pretty or be a big star or both. Heck, any guy who can string two sentences together and look good at the same time can be a sportscaster.
Jim Bouton

On BBC Radio cricket commentator John Arlott – John Arlott sounds like Uncle Tom Cobleigh reading Neville Cardus to the Indians.
Dylan Thomas

On BBC TV cricket commentator Richie Benaud – Richie Benaud simply says 'out' with the grisly finality of the hangman.
Tony Brace

A leg cutter is a delivery which batsmen play and miss at outside off-stump when Richie Benaud is commentating.
Vic Marks

On BBC Radio cricket commentator Henry Blofeld – An image persists of Henry Blofeld cracking champagne bottles and entertaining blondes until the early hours, and arriving late at the game with a stinking headache. Really, of course, he snuggles up every night with a hot water bottle, reading one of the novels of William Makepiece Thackeray.
Peter Roebuck *Tangled up in White* **(1990)**

On Match of the Day *expert Trevor Brooking* – England's most cultured ex-midfielder and now leading BBC television barbiturate … he still manages to make Nigel Mansell sound like Murray Walker on acid. And he looks like Virginia Wade.
Elf **(1993)**

On US TV basketball commentator Hubie Brown – Hubie was to network ratings what the 'Titanic' was to the winter cruise business.
Pat Williams

To BBC TV boxing commentator Harry Carpenter – Harry, you're not as dumb as you look.

Muhammad Ali (1972)

On BBC TV commentator David Coleman – Watching the BBC is something deeper, something occult, something to do with David Coleman's personality. Just by being so madly keen, he helps you get things in proportion. Anything that matters so much to David Coleman, you realise, doesn't matter so much at all.

Clive James *The Observer* **(1978)**

I am organising an expedition to discover the whereabouts of David Coleman. For some time now, the BBC have only been using repeats of his voice. No one can deny David is unique and that our children are now being corrupted by the occasional use of five-letter words. If educationalists are to gain influence over BBC Sport and allow the use of good English again, we will be forced into a literate Minister of Sport.

Private Eye (1976)

What is the most popular sport in Britain today?
a. darts
b. fishing
c. betting
d. travelling on the Tube without a ticket
e. sports quizzes
f. making up remarks supposed to have been said by David Coleman?

Miles Kington

On US TV sportscaster Howard Cosell – A voice that had all the resonance of a clogged Dristan bottle.

Encyclopaedia Britannica Year Book **(1973)**

Sometimes Howard makes me wish I was a dog and he was a fireplug.

Muhammad Ali

In one year I travelled 450,000 miles by air. That's about 18 and a half times around the world or once around Howard Cosell's head.

Jackie Stewart

On US TV baseball analyst Joe Garagiola – Joe Garagiola is considered a humorist like Mark Twain, who also came from Missouri. The resemblance is purely residential.

Jim Brosnan

On ITV football expert Jimmy Greaves – A walrus in a woolly jumper, affected his customary objectionable they-call-me-Joe-Blunt persona ... spoke fluent bilge. In short, he was as illuminating as the average taxi driver, without the saving grace of getting you anywhere.

Victor Lewis-Smith *Evening Standard* **(1992)**

On BBC TV sports commentator and presenter Tony Gubba – Try to imagine Frank Bough in utero and what do you get? Tony Gubba, of course.

Julian Barnes (1977)

On Match of the Day *expert Alan Hansen* – Thunderbirds *puppet who's now made a career out of bleating on and on about Liverpool's injury problems on* Match of the Day. Was never exactly Mr Controversial in his playing days – and same can be said of his TV career. His strong accent is a problem, but viewers should be able to understand him better when he finally manages to extricate his tongue from Bob Wilson's arse.

Zit (1993)

Alan Hansen and Gary Lineker are Mr and Mrs Mogadon.

Zit (1993)

On BBC TV football expert Jimmy Hill – I don't think there's much doubt about who's the smuggest among football's TV stars. Yes, it's Jimmy Hill … Take that chin away to the Natural History Museum, where it belongs.

When Saturday Comes

In *Match of the Day*, Jimmy Hill does his modern version of that favourite medieval theological exercise – debating how many angels could sit on the head of a pin. But with him, it's called 'Did he fall or was he pushed?' It involves slow motion, psychology, and elementary physics, and is conducted with such straight-faced fervour that it is hard to remember that he is talking of the momentary grounding of a gladiator rather than the downfall of empires.

Shaun Usher *Daily Mail* (1975)

Possibly over-estimating his own appeal – I'm sure people would rather hear me talking about football than someone like Ian Wright.

Jimmy Hill (1995)

On BBC Radio cricket commentator Brian Johnston – He was a man whose personal church clock stood perpetually at ten to three, and for whom there was always honey for tea. Not just honey either: cream cake and sponge cake and cherry cake and Dundee cake and walnut cake … Johnston's enduring contribution to Western civilisation is the cake-by-cake commentary.

The Times obituary (1994)

On Brian Johnston – A Kipling on laughing gas.

Tom Hiney *Modern Review* (1994)

In the light of the previous obit notice, surely a 'Mr Kipling' on laughing gas?

Colin M. Jarman

On Sky Sports presenter Richard Keys – A presenter with a dinky Sky logo on his blazer presides over the grim revelry with a fixed, moronic grin. It is a vision of holiday camp hell.

Tony Parsons *The Observer* (1992)

There's a simple recipe about this sports business. If you're a sporting star, you're a sporting star. If you don't quite make it you become a coach. If you can't coach, you become a journalist. If you can't spell, you introduce *Grandstand* on a Saturday afternoon.

Desmond Lynam, BBC TV sports presenter

Desmond Lynam is so laid back he's almost horizontal – which is exactly how his legions of fantasising housewifely fans imagine him to be.

Frank Keating

On US TV sports presenter Tim McCarver – McCarver is the pre-eminent over-analyst of his day. Ask him what time it is, and he'll tell you how a watch works. He can do 20 minutes on the height of infield grass.

Norman Chad *Sports Illustrated* (1992)

On BBC TV golf commentator Mark McCormack – 'Faldo's looking disconsolate,' McCormack observed. He might have added that Norfolk's looking flat. Euphemism is the stock-in-trade of the commentary box. 'Beautifully judged' denotes any shot that lands within 15 yards of the hole, where it automatically becomes a 'birdie opportoonity'. Other phrases to watch: 'Underclubbed' (the idiot didn't hit the ball far enough); 'he'll be disappointed with that' (wild hook into the grandstand); 'he'll be very disappointed with that' (old lady in hospital); and 'I wonder what's going through his mind?' (not a lot, the miserable sod).

Kenneth Roy *The Observer* (1995)

On Channel 4 TV horse racing analyst John McCririck – People like John McCririck are blind. They've never sat on a horse in their life. They wouldn't know a horse if it kicked them.

Charlie Brooks, BBC Radio 5 (1994)

John McCririck … looking a like a hedge dragged through a man backwards.

Sunday Express (1994)

Ninety-four per cent of Channel 4 viewers think that John McCririck's hand-wavings are a load of b*ll**ks.

Jo Brand *Brain Drain* BBC 2 (1993)

He reckons he's a sexual athlete. But the bejewelled, arm-waving John McCririck looks more like a beached whale than a good bet between the sheets.

Carole Malone *Daily Star* (1994)

On Daily Telegraph horse racing correspondent J. A. McGrath – He calls himself 'Hotspur', a nom de plume that is for some reason considered less silly than Crystal Palace or Brighton and Hove Albion.

Marcus Berkmann *Punch* (1993)

On Channel 4 TV horse racing presenter Jim McGrath – A personable form expert whose relaxed charm is belied by his staring eyes. He looks like a missionary, the kind of chap who might show up on your doorstep to persuade you to join the Temple of Temperate Tipsters. When McGrath recommends a horse, you *believe.*

Andrew Baker *Independent on Sunday* (1996)

On US TV American Football commentator John Madden – John is one man who doesn't let success go to his clothes.

Mike Ditka

On BBC Radio cricket commentator Christopher Martin-Jenkins – Born with a diamond-encrusted golden spoon thrust well down the throat.

Don Mosey *The Alderman's Tale* (1991)

Christopher Martin-Jenkins and Neil Durden-Smith were standing there next to the bar skittles, playing with each others' hyphens.

Peter Tinniswood *Tales from Whitney Scrotum*

On BBC TV tennis commentator Dan Maskell – During the course of Wimbledon, Dan Maskell said 'Ooh, I say' a total of 1,368 times. The trouble with Dan's style is that it's so infectious. Ooh I say, it's a really infectious style.

Clive James (1978)

On ITV football commentator Brian Moore – The only man alive today who was already bald when Bobby Charlton wasn't.

Bill Matthews *Punch* (1989)

Brian Moore is the only person who polishes his head before appearing on TV.

When Saturday Comes

On BBC TV football commentator John Motson – His career could only really be enhanced by a laryngectomy.

Matthew Norman *Evening Standard* (1994)

Known affectionately as Motty, John Motson would be better dubbed Motto as his commentary style draws heavily on the kind of homilies normally confined to Christmas crackers.

Allison Pearson *Independent on Sunday* (1994)

On ITV sports reporter Gary Newbon – If Gary Newbon were made of chocolate, he'd eat himself.

Reg Gutteridge (1991)

On Channel 4 TV horse racing presenter Lord John Oaksey – Given the choice between a vasectomy without an anaesthetic, and listening to Lord Oaksey ramble on about past Whitbread Gold Cups on the *Morning Line*, I would make the former a shade of odds on.

Mark Winstanley *Sporting Life* (1994)

Addressed to John Oaksey – Dear Bastard, you could not tip more rubbish if London Weekend bought you a fork-lift truck.

Letter to *Daily Telegraph*

On BBC TV horse racing commentator Peter O'Sullevan – Had he been at Balaclava he would have kept pace with the Charge of the Light Brigade in precise order and described the riders' injuries before they hit the ground.

Hugh McIlvanney *The Observer* (1977)

On BBC TV athletics commentator Ron Pickering – Ron continued to overheat as usual. The mockery of my confreres had chided him out of saying 'He's pulling out the big one', and even 'He's whacking in the big one'; but the National Viewers' and Listeners' Association will cut off his tail with a carving knife for his new and shameful variant: 'If she hits the board and bangs a big one, that'll put her in the bronze medal position.'
Julian Barnes New Statesman (1978)

On BBC TV Fantasy Football League's 'Statto' (aka Angus Loughran) – Statto is the Pat Coombs of Fantasy Football.
Herring & Norman Evening Standard

On US TV football and golf commentator Pat Summerall – If I ever got cancer, I would want Pat Summerall to be the one to tell me.
Beano Cook

On US TV basketball commentator Dick Vitale – His voice could peel the skin off a potato.
Norman Chad Washington Post

On BBC TV motor racing commentator Murray Walker – Even in moments of tranquillity, Murray Walker sounds like a man whose trousers are on fire.
Clive James Glued to the Box

After the BBC lost the Grand Prix motor racing TV rights to ITV – THERE goes the job! THERE goes the pension rights. THERE goes the share options, and THERE goes the air miles.
Rory Bremner Apparently Channel 4 TV (1995)

On BBC TV rugby league commentator Eddie Waring – Eddie Waring has done as much for Rugby League as Cyril Smith would do for hang-gliding.
Reg Bowden

On TV football presenter Bob Wilson – He just about sums Arsenal up – the verbal equivalent of a square ball across the back four. Watching him trying to make Football Focus entertaining is like watching Doug Rougvie dribble – a painful experience.
When Saturday Comes

On BBC TV horse racing presenter Julian Wilson – Why does Julian Wilson have to say 'orf' in the review of a race? Orf is a disease which affects sheep.
Peter Wilson (1993)

On his BBC TV partnership with Gerry Williams at Wimbledon – I like to think we're Saint and Greavsie with completed sentences.
Des Lynam (1987)

Media Speak

Nobody I've ever played with has said 'Sick as a parrot' when I've asked them how they were. But thrust a microphone in front of them, and it all comes out, 'It was a game of two halves', 'We'll take each match as it comes', 'The boy done good.' We have caught it from them – we're as sick as a commentator.
Gary Lineker (1990)

Football phrases from Regnar's Thesaurus ... he became, if not master, then an aspiring student of the synonym. On his great days he could avoid using the precise word throughout the duration of a report. He was a man of his time; he never in his life referred to a match as a 'clash'; and only rarely as a 'match'; it was a 'derby', 'duel', 'contest', 'tourney', 'battle', 'renewal of hostilities', 'struggle' ('epic' or, at best, 'titanic'). It was almost unknown for one of his players to shoot or head a goal. They 'drove home', 'converted', 'nodded', 'equalised', 'notched', 'reduced the leeway', 'increased the advantage', 'applied the finishing touch' or 'left the custodian helpless'.

John Arlott *The Guardian* **(1972)**

In other sports, the lateral euphemism is still in its infancy (at Wimbledon, for example, they have only just realised that 'perfectionist' can be used to represent 'extremely bad-tempered'). In soccer, the form of the extended adjective is well defined, 'tenacious', for example, always means 'small'.

Julian Barnes *The Observer* **(1992)**

Teams don't lose, they 'crash' or 'slump' to defeat. Goalkeepers who don't let any goals in have 'clean sheets', which presumably saves on detergent. And managers do not buy players, they 'splash out' on them, although whether they do so on a 'clean sheet' is rarely specified.

Marcus Berkmann *Punch* **(1993)**

The only word never used to describe what happens in football is 'kick'. The ball is always 'volleyed' or 'struck' or 'driven'. 'Kick' only happens when players do it to each other.

Penelope Gilliat *The Guardian* **(1974)**

The TV football analysts' seasonal scuffle with the English language continues: 'scores' continue to be 'scorelines', tackles to be 'scything'. The factotum adverb 'well' (Hibbitt did well, didn't he do well, oh he did do well). If a player isn't doing well, or does something badly, he is invariably described as unlucky: 'he was very unlucky there', or simply 'oh ... unlucky'.

Martin Amis (1975)

As cricket surges down the years, the mathematical cherish its statistics. But the literary relish its sharp Saxon vocab: drive, block, cut, glance, pull, spin, toss, lob, swing, not to mention its silly mid-off and deep square legs.

John F. X. Harriott (1976)

In an attempt to glamorise a dying industry, the sports dictionary has been turned upside down; centre-forwards are strikers, throw-ins are set pieces, the pitch is now the park. In racing, grooms are calling themselves trainers, and when a horse is referred to as an in-and-out performer, it means it only wins when the stable has backed it. And a racing correspondent is now a would-be gentleman without a private income.

Jeffrey Bernard (1975)

AND FINALLY ...

The opera isn't over till the fat lady sings.
Dick Motta, Washington Bullets basketball coach

Where does this saying, a favourite of sportscasters, come from? Well, what ain't over is an opera, Wagner's *Siegfried*; and the fat lady is Brunnhilde. By 11.30 Siegfried makes it up to the mountain top, right through the impenetrable fire. He finds Brunnhilde and removes the breastplate from the almost-certainly amplitudinous body of the Wagnerian soprano who sleeps under it. What he says, with gargantuan understatement, is, *Das ist kein Mann* (That is no man).
Anyway, at about 11.40, Brunnhilde starts to sing. Vocally, she's fresh as a daisy. Siegfried, who's been singing non-stop since seven, must join in for a final love duet of Promethean difficulty, which ends, along with the opera, at 12.20.
Anthony Tommasini *Boston Globe* (1990)

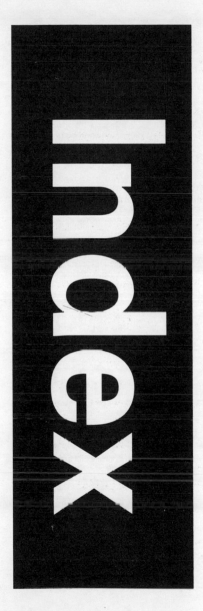